Being a Christian in the Wesleyan Traditon

D0777537

Being a Christian in the Wesleyan Traditon

Belonging, Believing, Living, Growing

JOHN O. GOOCH

DISCIPLESHIP RESOURCES

PO BOX 340003 • NASHVILLE, TN 37203-0003
www.discipleshipresources.org

ISBN 978-0-88177-559-4

Library of Congress Control Number 2009923906

Table of Contents

. . . .

Preface

· ·

This book began in an email from the editor, George Donigian, who said, "We need a new membership manual for adults in the United Methodist Church. Are you interested in writing one?" Quite honestly, I was not. Fortunately, at the end of the email George said something like, "I already don't like what I said. Let's do something different. Send me a proposal about what you think adults need to know to help them grow in their faith and in understanding of The United Methodist Church." *That* I liked.

With a background in youth ministry, I knew something about taking risks. With a background in pastoring United Methodist churches, I knew something about the kinds of questions people asked about the church. As a church historian, I thought I knew something about John Wesley and the development of our denomination. With that background—or, rather, those backgrounds—I set out to write. And what fun I had writing it.! My fingers flew across the keyboard on the first drafts.

I was born and raised in the Methodist church and, now, the United Methodist church. The church nurtured me, gave me hope, brought me to despair, loved me, gave me opportunities to do exciting things, and wore me out. I love the United Methodist Church in spite of itself, because of all that she has given me. So I began thinking about how to translate that love into words.

I believe that the church is about belonging, believing, growing, and living. So those are the sections into which the book is divided. I put belonging first, because my experience says that, in today's world, most of us belong before we believe. When we believe and commit ourselves to Jesus Christ and to the church, we begin to grow in our faith and our understanding of how faith influences daily life. Then we are faced with the questions about how we live out our faith in a confusing, sometimes hostile, world. Each of the main sections has several chapters, and each chapter deals with one specific sub-topic of the section. At the end of each section you'll find both questions for reflection (ranging from "relatively easy" to "wrestling match" level!) and some suggestions for further reading.

As you spend some time with the book, you will be faced with questions and decisions about what it means to be a Christian disciple in the United Methodist tradition. Our tradition is not necessarily better than others, but it is our tradition. It is important that we know who we are, from where we came, and how we do mission, ministry, and theology in the world. You will discover that there are important differences between United Methodists and other denominations. Those differences don't make us better, but they do make us unique. May you have great joy—and a deeper faith—as you wrestle with the differences.

John O. Gooch
Liberty, MO

Section I

Belonging

1

Do You Belong?

• •

"I don't want to have anything to do with the church. I had enough of that when I was a kid and my folks dragged me to Sunday School and worship and potlucks and all kinds of things. People were such hypocrites. They talked about love and then sniped at each other, and didn't have any time for us kids. I believe in God and consider myself a spiritual person. I'll just deal with that personally and you can keep the church, thank you very much."

"Church people are so narrow-minded and judgmental. If you don't measure up to some standard they set, you are made to feel like an outcast. If churches only practiced the love and openness they talk about, I might be interested. But until then I'll keep on living my spirituality without any help from them."

" I went to church a few times, but all they ever talked about was the institution. They needed money to build a new building. They needed volunteers to teach Sunday School. They needed people to sign up for the church supper. The choir needed new robes. I thought the church was supposed to be about helping people live better lives. I can do that on my own. I don't need the new choir robes to be a Christian. "

" I spend time each week outdoors, enjoying the beauty of the natural world. Most of the time I can find a quiet spot where I can sit and reflect on life and God and how I relate to God. I'm a spiritual person, and think I have a pretty good relationship with God. Isn't that enough for anyone? "

Those are some of the living voices of "Spirituality Without Religion." They have it just right on one point: The church doesn't always live up to its ideals. There are hypocrites and narrow-minded, judgmental people and an emphasis on the institution. That happens whenever any group of people comes together. But there is another side to the church as well. This view says that the church is an organized religious body that offers relationship with God within a community of people searching for God. It offers spiritual growth, meaning for life, and an authentic moral existence. It is a body that challenges us to be better than we are, gives us support in our struggles, and holds us accountable for our failures. The "religion" part of "spirituality without religion" offers us an organization in which those things happen and clarifies the "spirituality" part by offering us a clear context and content for our spirituality.

There is something about us that wants to belong. Our very nature seems to put a high value on belonging. In elementary school, we don't want to be the last one chosen for the team. We want to be with our close friends, that little pack of kids whose company and approval we need to have. If we are separated from them, perhaps because some of them are put in another section of our grade at school, we are devastated and sure that we can't function in school at all. In high school, we want to make the team, or the band, or the cheerleading squad. Whoever we are, we want to be "tight" with other kids like us, who have the same interests and values. Sometimes those kids are in youth group at church, sometimes they are the computer club, or the cross-country team, or the college bowl team. In college, we want to belong to the right fraternity or sorority. Or we want to belong to the football team, the honor societies, whatever group it is that expresses who we are, what we want to become, how we want to be seen by others. In short, we want to belong.

Belonging helps us identify who we are. "I'm a Rotarian (Mason, Elk, PEO)," we say. That helps people know something about us. We are known by the company we keep. Belonging also makes us part of something bigger than ourselves. When we belong to a group, we do not belong just to the present manifestation of the group. We belong to all that went before, to the history and tradition of the group. We identify with the founders, with the "heroes and heroines" who have helped make the group what it is. We identify with the ideals, the goals, the practical challenges that the group takes on. The Lions, for example, are known for collecting eyeglasses and distributing them to persons who need glasses but can't afford them. Rotarians are best known for their work in polio eradication. When we belong to one of those groups, we take up the challenge of working toward those goals. And we help, consciously or unconsciously, to mold the future of the group. We also, for better or worse, belong to the "warts" of the organization, its flaws and failings.

This is what it's like to belong to the church. We sign up with the present, with a particular congregation. But we also sign on to the inheritance of the congregation. We become a part of the heritage of the faith that stretches from Abraham and Sarah to the present. That's almost 4,000 years of tradition! We become a part of the work of God in Moses, David, Isaiah, Jeremiah, and the other prophets. We become part of the work of God in Jesus of Nazareth, in Peter and Paul and Mary Magdalene and all the other early disciples. Our heritage includes all that happened in the church for 2,000 years. And we identify with the founders and the leaders of our own United Methodist Church. We also become a part of the heritage of the local congregation. In some local churches, that means becoming a part of up to 200 years of tradition and service. In other churches, it may mean sharing the experience of meeting at the local school or theater until a building can be built for the congregation. In the latter case, we build a great deal of the heritage ourselves.

The reality is that, for the most part, we belong before we believe. A person can be a member of a service club for years before, one day, it finally hits them what the idea of service is all about. Someone can be a member of a church for years before he or she really believes in Jesus Christ and makes a commitment to what the church stands for in the community and the world. This simple belonging without commitment can be a fact of life both for persons who were born into the church and for those who discovered the church as adults.

In this section, we will talk about the details of belonging, and what it means on the surface to be a United Methodist. In later sections, we will deal with belief and the implications of growing in faith.

2

Where Did We Come From?

● ●

The answer to that question is a lengthy book in itself. Some excellent books have been written to answer it, several of them are listed at the end of this section. To radically over-simplify, we can say that we come from several sources. One, of course, is the Methodist movement started by John Wesley that flourished in America under the leadership of Francis Asbury. Another is The United Brethren, a primarily German-speaking group influenced by Wesley, and always in touch with the Methodists, but with some serious differences in theology as well as language. A third is the Evangelical Association, another German-speaking group, again influenced by Wesley's writing.

There were also major divisions with Methodism, so that we have Free Methodists, the Methodist Episcopal Church, the Methodist Episcopal Church South, the Methodist Protestants, and many other groups. In addition, there are three African-American Methodist denominations—the African Methodist Episcopal Church, the African Methodist Episcopal Zion Church, and the Christian Methodist Episcopal Church.

16

Over the years, several of these denominations have come together and the result is what we now call the United Methodist Church. For purposes of historical reference, we will call the predecessors of the United Methodist Church by their historic names, without intending to slight anyone who comes from a different part of our heritage.

That said, there are some key persons and events in our history that are foundational for knowing "where we came from." If United Methodists had trading cards, such as we find in baseball, football, and other sports, these are some of the people and events that might appear on them.

JOHN WESLEY

Our story begins with a priest in the Church of England who was searching for the peace of God in his heart. His name was John Wesley (1703-1791), and he was a professor at Oxford, missionary to America, writer, publisher, experimenter with electricity, educator, social service pioneer, worker for justice, advocate for the poor, and leader of the evangelical revival in England. His search for God is a reminder for all of us that even the saints struggle. Out of his work as a revival preacher and justice advocate came the Methodist movement, of which we are a part. Wesley did not intend to start a new church, but only to reform the Church of England. Only after the American Revolution did he make plans for a separate church in America.

CHARLES WESLEY

John's "baby brother," who also became a leader in the revival. His greatest contribution was in the hymns he wrote. Though some of his poems and hymns were pretty ordinary, others are among the greatest ever written. The ones with which we are probably most familiar are "Hark! The Herald Angels Sing" and "Christ the Lord is Risen Today." He also wrote the "Methodist anthem," the hymn, "O, For a Thousand Tongues to Sing."

His son and grandsons were also great musicians.

THE HOLY CLUB

Can you imagine belonging to a group at college called the "Holy Club"? The name was not one chosen by the people in the group, but was a derogatory name given by those who made fun of them. The Holy Club was a small group of students, under the leadership of Charles Wesley, who asked John to be their "faculty advisor" and their spiritual guide. They met regularly for prayer and Bible study, and devoted themselves to good works—visiting the sick and those in prison, finding a teacher for poor children, finding food for the hungry and medicine for the sick. Out of their work came key parts of the Wesleyan Revival in England, particularly the work with the poor and dispossessed.

SUSANNA WESLEY

The mother of John and Charles (and 17 other children, 11 of whom survived to adulthood.) The wife of an Anglican clergyman, she taught her children at home. They learned spiritual disciplines as well as reading and writing, and Susanna made time for each of them each week to check on their spiritual growth. She was a great influence on John both theologically and practically. On more than one occasion, she cautioned him not to act rashly on an issue. Her wisdom helped lead to more than one significant development in the Methodist movement. She is our honored foremother.

FRANCIS ASBURY

A lay preacher and missionary to America. During the Revolution, he was one of the few Wesleyan preachers who stayed in America. After the war, he was appointed by Wesley and elected by the preachers to become the head of the American church. This was the first actual founding of a Methodist denomination. Bishop Asbury led the church through its difficult formative years and laid the foundations for the great church that Methodism became. He rode his horse hundreds of thousands of miles, preaching, organizing the church, and encouraging the new classes formed on the frontier.

THE CHRISTMAS CONFERENCE

Wesley appointed Asbury to lead the American church, but Asbury wanted to be elected by the preachers. At Christmas time in 1789 the preachers came together, ordained Asbury, elected him and Thomas Coke as bishops, and organized the Methodist Episcopal Church. This conference marks the official beginning of The Methodist Episcopal Church in America.

PHILIP WILLIAM OTTERBEIN

A German immigrant who was pastor of the German Evangelical Reformed Church in Baltimore, Maryland, where he served from 1774 to 1813. At a revival meeting held in a barn near Lancaster, PA., he heard Martin Boehm (see below) preach and exclaimed to him afterward, "Wir sind Bruder" (We are brethren). This meeting was one of the events that led to the United Brethren as a denomination. Otterbein was a friend of Francis Asbury, and the common emphasis on personal religious experience brought them even closer. Otterbein was, in fact, one of the pastors who laid hands on Asbury at his ordination.

MARTIN BOEHM

Boehm was a Mennonite lay preacher who was also deeply influenced by the writings of John Wesley. About 1775 he broke with the Mennonites, and in 1789 and 1791 held joint conferences with Otterbein and others, leading to the formation of the United Brethren.

The United Brethren were a German speaking denomination for the early part of its history.

JACOB ALBRIGHT

Albright was a Revolutionary War veteran who was deeply shocked by the deaths of three of his children in a dysentery epidemic. As he struggled with his grief and why God would allow that to happen, he was converted and joined a Methodist class meeting. In 1796 he began preaching. He later formed the classes he organized into an independent organization called Albright's People. This was the beginning of the Evangelical Association, another group of primarily German ancestry that is a rich part of our heritage.

RICHARD ALLEN

Allen was a former slave who had purchased his freedom and rose to prominence as the first bishop of the African Methodist Episcopal Church. He belonged to St. George's Church in Philadelphia. St. George's was an integrated church, and Africans worshiped there freely before 1787. In 1787, a series of events, beginning with segregating black members to the balcony, and ending with two white trustees of the church trying to pull black worshippers from their knees in prayer, led to a walkout of African members. They began to worship separately and in 1794, Asbury dedicated a building for their use. This was

"Mother Bethel" church. Discrimination continued in struggles over the property and Allen and others joined together to organize the A.M.E. church, which continues to be an important part of the American Methodist scene today.

CIRCUIT RIDERS

Early Methodist preachers did not settle down and serve a church in a town. Instead, they covered vast distances on horseback, covering their "circuits" on the frontier. The circuits were huge. Joseph Oglesby, for example, was appointed to "Illinois" in 1804. These circuit riders preached wherever they could find a group of settlers, and were responsible for seeking out families on the frontier, organizing classes, and providing the sacraments to their people. Because of their efforts, Methodism became the dominant church on the frontier. Circuit riders were also responsible for helping develop public morality and justice across the frontier.

SLAVERY AND DIVISION

Not all of our United Methodist "trading cards" give us great pride. Methodists struggled with the question of slavery from the very beginning. The church condemned the practice in theory, but was never able to enforce their teaching, because of the resistance of slave-owners. After years of bitter fighting over the issue, the General Conference of 1844 provided for a division in the church, along the lines of free and slave areas of the United States. The result of this division was the separate Methodist Episcopal Church and the Methodist Episcopal Church, South. It was not until 1939 that the wounds of division, war, and reconstruction healed enough that the separate branches came back together.

FRANCES WILLARD

In the late nineteenth century when women were not considered the equal of men and were denied seats in the annual and general conferences of The Methodist Church, Frances Willard led the fight for the full inclusion of women. She was elected to more than one General Conference that refused to seat her, but the day finally came when women took their rightful place in the conference. Willard was also an early leader in the Women's Christian Temperance Union, which led the fight against alcohol abuse.

WORLD MISSION

From its earliest days, American Methodism (and Evangelicals and United Brethren) believed in the call to reach out to those who had not heard the gospel. At first, this was a mission to the American frontier, where the circuit riders helped bring both the Christian faith and social order to frontier society. Then the first missionary went to Liberia and the world mission was born. Soon, there were missions in India, Africa, China, South America, in almost all the world. Missionaries taught schools; founded universities, hospitals, and medical clinics; brought the gospel to the masses and founded churches, fought for social justice; and changed the world.

THE SOCIAL CREED

John Wesley had taught there was no holiness except social holiness, and his followers sought to change society in ways that would bring in the kingdom of God. In 1905, the Methodist Episcopal Church developed the first "Social Creed," a statement about the way in which the gospel spoke to the secular world. The emphasis in that first statement was on the right of labor to bargain collectively. Today the Social Principles is a substantial document, addressing a wide range of issues that confront the world.

3

What's the Secret Handshake?

● ●

When I became a Boy Scout in the sixth grade, one of the first things I learned was the "scout handshake." It was unique, totally unlike any other handshake I was ever likely to use. Other organizations have "secret" handshakes that only members can know. In those organizations, one knows other members by the way they respond to the secret handshake.

United Methodism doesn't have anything like a secret handshake, but there are certain things that help identify who we are and the things for which we stand. In that category, we include such things as:

- Infant baptism
- Open communion
- Connectionalism
- Apportionments
- The appointment system

Let's look at each of those briefly, to see why they are distinctive, and how they identify us almost automatically as United Methodists.

United Methodists—and the denominations that later became United Methodists—have always been identified by *baptism.* On the American frontier, where Methodists flourished, we were known as those crazy people who baptized babies. That set us apart from the Baptists, Disciples, and others who were also active on the frontier. Part of the reason we baptize babies is our tradition. We come out of the Church of England, which baptized babies as a matter of course. That's our heritage, and we continue the practices of our ancestors. But a larger part of the reason why we baptize babies has to do with the way we look at the relationship among God, the church, and the individual believer. Some other denominations believe that only adults should be baptized, because only they can make a decision about their relationship to God. United Methodists believe that children and infants should be baptized, because that brings them into the heritage, the community, the faith of the church. It then becomes the responsibility of the whole church to help them grow in the faith, so that they can one day own for themselves that which their parents and the congregation have claimed for them. In the "Believing" section we'll talk more about how this understanding of baptism. For now, it's enough to know that infant baptism is part of the "secret handshake" that makes United Methodists who we are.

Open communion is also a key mark of United Methodists. At least some other denominations believe that, in order to receive communion, one must be an adult member of the church. Further, a member of that particular denomination—in extreme cases, a member of that congregation. For United Methodists, open communion means that anyone is welcome at the Lord's table, regardless of age or church affiliation. Again, we'll talk about this in more detail in the "Believing" section, but it's important to know here that all are welcome at the Lord's table in United Methodism. In the old ritual, the words of invitation said, "Ye that do truly and earnestly repent of your sins, and are in love and charity with your neighbors, and intend to lead a new life. . . ." The key was the openness to God in Jesus Christ and the intention to change one's life. Today, a pastor will often say words such as "this is a United Methodist service, but it is the Lord's table. Everyone who would like a new or deeper relationship with Jesus Christ is invited." There are important theological reasons for this open invitation, which will be discussed in detail in Section II: Believing. One practical application is that United Methodists invite to the table children of all ages.

The connection is a key part of becoming a United Methodist. We belong to something bigger than the local congregation. We are a part of all United Methodists, our congregations, agencies, missions, everywhere in the world. We identify with the glories and successes of the connection—and we live with its faults and failures as well. Originally, the "connection" was a group of preachers in England who were "in connection with Mr. Wesley." In that early sense, the connection was a network. But it was also more than a network. It was a system of support and accountability. The preachers supported each other in their work—and they held each other accountable for a high standard of discipline and living in the world. The connection worked among the Methodists in England, but it really "took off" on the American frontier. The system of discipline and accountability, the system of appointments (see below) and the ability of the preachers to adapt to changing conditions helped make Methodism the major Protestant body in America. In our

day, the connection is still a network of relationships among
individuals, congregations, conferences, and agencies. As a connection, we share a common vision, we hold the same
memories of the past, live under the same discipline, and come
together for planning specific ways to help our vision become
an expression of the kingdom of God on earth. In the connection we also share our resources and leadership. An important
part of the connection is a collection of agencies made up of
leaders in the fields of education, evangelism, social justice, mission, and other specialties who provide leadership, training,
and resources for the churches in the connection.

We see the connection in concrete form primarily in two
ways: the *appointment* system and *apportionments*. United
Methodist churches do not "call" pastors, though they consult
with the church leadership about who their pastor will be.
Instead, pastors are appointed to local churches by the bishop,
to serve a term of one year. At the end of that year, they may be
re-appointed to that congregation, in fact probably will be. But
they may also be moved to another congregation where the
bishop and his or her advisors believe their gifts best match the
needs of the church. There is good news and bad news in the
appointment system. The good news is that United Methodist
churches always have a pastor. Maybe not always the pastor they
want, but a pastor. Churches are not left to struggle on their
own. At one point, I served in the same small county seat town
for eight years. During that eight years, the Presbyterians, who
operate under the call system, were without a pastor for five. I
provided pastoral care for the Presbyterian congregation to
some degree, but they were without a pastor/preacher who
would be in the pulpit each Sunday, care for the sick, baptize
babies, perform weddings, administer the Sacrament, and offi-
ciate at funerals. At the end of that time, one Methodist (as we

were called then) layman said to me, "I never believed in the appointment system until now." So what's the bad news? Well, your congregation may have a pastor you love who is moved by the bishop to another church. You don't want that to happen, but you don't have much choice. Or, you may have a pastor you really don't like, but you can't get the bishop to move him/her and send you another pastor.

The other way the connection expresses itself is in the form of *apportionments.* United Methodists have a wide range of agencies and missions, and those cost money to operate. We're all in it together (that's one thing connection means) and so we all "chip in" every year to help pay the bills. Each local church is assigned a specific amount, based on a formula that tries to treat each church fairly depending on its size and ability to pay. We don't always like the apportionments, and many congregations refuse to pay them, or pay them only under protest. But, hey, that's a part of what it means to be a United Methodist and "in connection" with all those other United Methodists. We truly "bear one another's burdens," including the cost of maintaining the denominational structure.

4

What Makes Us Special?

• •

Have you noticed? Every activity seems to have its own special language. If you get into computers, you learn about gigabytes, websites, and so on. In football, the language is draw plays and "cover two." (I have no idea what a "cover two" defense is.) In music, the special language is actually Italian, but you have to figure out what each word is telling you to do. And don't even think about physics! The same is true with Christian faith. We have our own special vocabulary, full of words such as justification, redemption, providence, and a host of other words. We'll focus more on that language in Section II, when we talk about believing. Here it's enough to say there are some special words and phrases that set United Methodists apart in the theological world. There really *is* a difference between denominations in terms of what they believe. We may all be headed toward the same goal—the kingdom of God—but we have different understandings about what it means to live as Christians toward that goal.

One key phrase that sets us apart is "Faith *and* Works." A quick look back at some of our common heritage shows us why this is important. At the time of the Protestant Reformation (the sixteenth century), reformers such as Martin Luther in Germany and John Calvin in Switzerland thought that the Roman Catholic Church was way over the line to believing that "works" brought about salvation. ("Works" meaning that if we just do enough good things and pile up enough spiritual brownie points, God will have to give us salvation.) Going to the other extreme, these reformers said that only God's grace (God's love for human beings, which is totally undeserved) accepted through faith, can save us. Their emphasis was on *sola gratia* (some of our special language is still Latin), *sola fide, sola Scriptura* (grace alone, faith alone, Scripture alone). That emphasis came as a response to what the Reformers perceived as the mistakes of the Roman Catholic Church, leaning too much toward human endeavors to bring about salvation.

John Wesley's position was more of a middle way. He said that both faith *and* works were important. He believed that we are saved by God's grace, accepted through faith. But he also believed that, because of that grace, we are called to live lives of honest effort to strengthen our relationship with God and serve our neighbors. The works that we do are, in part, a response to God's grace. Works are also a kind of preparation for receiving God's grace. We do the best we can to love God and our neighbors, and to work for justice and mercy in the world. This becomes a way of opening our lives to God. Today, United Methodists still live out the concept of faith and works.

Another key phrase is Scripture *and* tradition. Again, the Protestant Reformers thought that the Roman church was too deeply dependent on the traditional teachings of the Church and did not pay enough attention to Scripture. So they said

Scripture *alone* is the basis of Christian faith and teaching. John Wesley again took a middle position. He said it that Scripture was essential. But Scripture was interpreted through the traditional teachings of the church. If someone came up with an interpretation of Scripture that sounded strange, and that no one had thought of in all the history of the church, check it out very carefully. We believe that the Holy Spirit was not only involved in the writing of Scripture, but also in its interpretation. If an interpretation had never been thought of in 2,000 years, it might not be of the Spirit. Plus, Wesley said, we have other God-given tools for understanding Scripture. One is our Christian experience. We interpret Scripture in the light of our own experience of God. For example, if our experience of God is a God of love and compassion, who cares for all God's children, and we find a passage in the Bible that is being interpreted to say that God is a God of vengeance, we might want to look at that interpretation carefully—in the light of our experience. Today, we might add to the concept of experience the insights that science has given us into the workings of God in the world. Understanding creation through astronomy, physics, genetics, evolution, biology, and other sciences help us see more clearly the work of God in creation. Finally, Wesley also said that we interpret Scripture in the light of reason. Does it make sense? Do all the things we say about Scripture hang together? God has given us the power of thinking about faith, and we ought not neglect that power as we seek for insights in Scripture.

And, last, a key word—sanctification (holiness). For United Methodists, this is not about perfectionism, where we never make mistakes, where we have the "perfect" body, or the "perfect" marriage, or the "perfect" job. For us, it's about a way of life, given to us by God. Sanctification is a gift from God, bestowed on us by grace. It is also a striving to become everything that God has created us to be. So, for each of us, it's different. But for all of us, sanctification (holiness) is a way of life. Holiness is the way we go about our daily lives—working, playing, being part of a family, a community, a church. Holiness is finding ways to live out God's call to discipleship, to wholeness of life. Holiness for Joe might mean working in the soup kitchen three nights a week. For Marlene, holiness is cheerfully caring for a bed-ridden aunt. For Vernon, holiness might mean being on the city council and working for a better community, while for Beth it means helping the elderly poor with their taxes. It's all about how we live—and a unique mark of what it means to be United Methodist.

5

What *Does* the Church Expect of Us?

● ●

For several years, I was the pastor of a rapidly-growing suburban church. We took in members right and left, and most of them were pretty clear about what they expected from the church. They had definite ideas about what the church should do for them and how they expected the church to live up to those ideas. We worked hard at meeting those expectations and, judging by the way we grew, we must have done a pretty good job. One week I decided I'd turn the tables and I wrote an article for the newsletter about what the church expected from its members. What I expected was an uproar of protest. What I got was a wave of "thank you"s. People said they were glad to hear what the church expected and were willing to try to live up to those expectations. So what does the church expect?

When we take vows of membership, that is, when we choose to belong, we say that we will support the church by our prayers, presence, gifts, and service. That's pretty straightforward.

Do we pray for the church? For the pastor? For the staff, if it's a large church? That's a key way we support the church—but beware! Praying that the church will be able to carry out a particular program may lead you to volunteering to work on that program. And that's as it should be. God has answered your prayer by providing the people to bring the program to reality—and one of those people was you! Sometimes we pray best by working to bring our prayers to fruition.

Are we present? Is worship an option for us, or do we consider that being in worship each Sunday is an important part of how we relate to God and to the community? I told my congregation that, in addition to presence in worship, I expected that they would also be present in Sunday School or some other form of ongoing learning, to help them grow in faith. After all, the one distinctive thing the church does that no other human institution does is worship. If we belong, if we have taken the name, "Christian," then we need to be engaged in the one distinctive thing the church does. Other institutions teach, but only the church teaches the content and meaning of the faith. We need to be present in at least one form of learning, so that we can continue to grow in faith.

It comes a shock to many people that the church has bills, just like any other institution. There are salaries, utilities, upkeep on property, resources, and apportionments to pay. Belonging also means that we commit ourselves to support the church with our gifts. We are called to give gladly and generously, according to our ability to give. The lay leader of the congregation I mentioned above believed that United Methodists should tithe, that is, give 10% of their income to the work of the church. He commented one week that we sure drove good cars on $20,000 a year, meaning that most of us could afford to give a lot more than $2,000 a year. That kind of challenge brought some people up short and led them to think again about the level of support they gave.

Giving also includes service, but the two are listed separately in the commitment question. Whether it's serving on a committee, singing in the choir, teaching Sunday School, cleaning up the kitchen after a church supper, working in outreach to the community, helping those in real need, whatever it is, belonging means that we also serve. We give of our time and talent to help the church help others. Serving also involves being aware of who we are and what gifts we have to offer. If we can't abide committee meetings, but love to work in the garden, helping with the church grounds will be a more joyful form of service than serving on the finance committee. If we can't carry a tune, we probably should not consider the choir as our avenue of service. On the other hand, sometimes there are tasks to be done that just have to be done, and we need to give ourselves to them as well. The congregation we now claim as a church home is getting ready for a "clean-up day." It's going to be a day of throwing out trash, sweeping and dusting, getting ready for the fall programs. This is not my thing. But I plan to be there, hopefully with the youth I teach, to do our part in caring for the church. That's a part of what it means to belong.

6

How Are We Organized?

We're organized a lot like the United States. We have a Constitution. We have an executive branch, a legislative branch, and a judicial branch. The executive branch is composed of the Bishops of the church, who are elected by the church to lead us. One is a Bishop for life, but a Bishop can serve in any one area for only a maximum of 12 years. Also in the executive branch are the general boards and agencies of the church, who provide resources, training, and guidance for the local congregations. The legislative branch is composed of the conferences. At the local church level, there is the charge conference, or church conference, which sets policy for the congregation, including both programs and budget. The annual conference is composed of representatives from all the congregations in a geographic area. The annual conference is composed of equal numbers of clergy and laity, who are chosen by the local churches to represent them. The work of the annual conference is to set policy for that geographic area, determine the budget, and carry out the programs of the general church.

The General Conference, which meets every four years, is composed of representatives elected by the annual conferences, again with clergy and laity in equal numbers. The General Conference sets policy, guidelines, and budget for the entire church—and it is the only body that can speak *for* the church. The judicial branch is made up of a single Judicial Council, elected by the General Conference. Its function is to pass on the constitutionality of the actions of the bishops and/or the conferences when asked.

Section I Questions for Reflection

1. To what other organizations do you belong? What does belonging to them mean to you?
2. What new understandings did you find in this section that you want to know more about?
3. What questions or disagreements do you have?
4. What will you do to learn more about those under-standings, questions, or disagreements?
5. In what ways does "Belonging" now have a deeper meaning for you?
6. What are your expectations of the church? That is, what do you see as the benefits of belonging?
7. What do you see that the church expects of you? Has anyone in your congregation spelled out those expectations for you?
8. How do you feel when other organizations tell you what is expected of you as a member?
9. How do you feel when the church tells you what is

expected of you as a member? Is there a difference in the way you feel? Why do you suppose that is?

10. How will you be more intentional about supporting the church with your prayers, presence, gifts, and service?

11. Would you like to know more about your heritage as a United Methodist? There are several books listed in "For Further Reading" that you might enjoy.

FOR FURTHER READING

Ferguson, Charles W. *Methodists and the Making of America: Organizing to Beat the Devil.* Austin, Texas: Eakin Press, 1983. An easy-to-read survey of the Methodist movements in America.

Gooch, John O. *John Wesley for the 21st Century.* Nashville: Discipleship Resources, 2006. A series of issues that lift up the relevance of Wesley's teaching for today.

Heitzenrater, Richard P. *Wesley and the People Called Methodists.* Nashville: Abingdon Press, 1995. Probably the best short history of John Wesley's life and the beginnings of Methodism.

Jones, Scott J. *United Methodist Doctrine: The Extreme Center.* Nashville: Abingdon Press, 2002. An excellent review of what it is that United Methodists believe and why they believe it. Attempts to steer a course between the extremes of different understandings of doctrine.

Yrigoyen, Charles Jr. *John Wesley; Holiness of Heart and Life.* Nashville: Abingdon Press, 1996. A study of Wesley from the standpoint of holiness, or sanctification.

Section II

Believing

· ·

7

"You Bet Your Life"

●●

So, I belong. But I'm not sure I'm a Christian. What comes
next? I hear people talking about "giving their lives to Jesus"
and "making a commitment to Christ." I'm not sure I've ever
done that. I don't think I'd even know how. What does it mean
to make a commitment to Christ?

Let's talk about that on two levels. First, the personal, emo-
tional level. This is where most people are when they say they
"give their lives to Jesus." And it comes in different ways for different people. For some, it's a high, almost exalted moment.
They feel a sense of intentionally giving themselves over to Jesus
Christ, asking him to come into their lives, to take control of
their lives, and to lead them to a new and better way of living.
Other people "give their lives to Jesus" out a sense of resigna-
tion, almost despair. This was my experience. I was frustrated,
depressed, unhappy. One night I said, "OK, I don't have any
control of my life. Please take it and do with it whatever you
want. I give up trying to do it myself." I can't say I felt a great
change, but I did have a sense of peace about who I was and

where I was headed. That was good news. Then I discovered that surrender to Christ was not a one-time thing, something that happened once-for-all. I had to do it over and over again. It's easy to get involved in so many things that we forget about a conscious relationship with God through Jesus Christ. So we (or at least I) have to consciously make the decision to open our lives to him day after day, week after week. We "bet our lives" that this is what will give meaning and joy and peace to our lives.

The second level is the liturgical level, one which all United Methodists share in common. The liturgy is Baptismal Covenant I, which we use for all persons making a public first commitment, or wanting to renew the vows they made earlier (or were made for them) in their baptism. There are four questions that the pastor asks the person making the commitment (or parents/sponsors, in the case of infants).

> On behalf of the whole church, I ask you:
> Do you renounce the spiritual forces of wickedness, reject
> the evil powers of this world, and repent of your sin?[1]

This first question puts the choice starkly between the forces of good (God in Jesus Christ) and the forces of evil. When we make a commitment to Jesus Christ, we begin by renouncing the powers of this world. Some people call those powers demonic, or the forces of Satan. Others call them oppression and dehumanization, for example. Whatever we choose to call the powers, we commit ourselves to no longer give allegiance or service to them, but to commit our loyalty to Jesus Christ. In addition, we pub-

---

1. All citations are from "Baptismal Covenant I," *The United Methodist Hymnal*. Nashville: The United Methodist Publishing House, 1989, p. 34.

licly repent of our sins (without having to name them all), with the implicit asking of forgiveness for our past.

> Do you accept the freedom and power God gives you to resist evil, injustice, and oppression in whatever forms they present themselves?

This is a radical commitment, when we consider it carefully. We commit ourselves to resist injustice, whether economic, social, racial, or political. We commit ourselves to resist oppression, whether it takes the form of dictators oppressing people who want to be free; economic systems oppressing the poor; or social systems oppressing persons who are of a different color, nationality, sexual orientation, or who come from another nation seeking political and/or economic freedom. We commit ourselves to resisting evil, in whatever form it presents itself. And we come to realize that simply protesting, for example, is not enough. It isn't enough to resist injustice and oppression—we need to find ways to build systems of justice and freedom in their place. In Sections III and IV, which deal with Growing and Living, we'll discuss these ideas in more detail and relate them to concepts of social holiness. That discussion will also help us see how justice and freedom are part of a wholistic approach to the Christian life.

Note also that we don't have to go out and do battle by ourselves. We have freedom and power to resist evil because God gives them to us. This is another example of grace (God's unconditional love) at work in human life.

> Do you confess Jesus Christ as your Savior, put your whole trust in his grace, and promise to serve him as your Lord, in union with the church which Christ has opened to people of all ages, nations, and races?

After committing ourselves to reject evil, accept freedom to resist injustice and oppression, there comes the moment of positive affirmation, when we publicly say that we accept Jesus Christ as our Savior. That means, as the following phrases say, that we trust him completely to save us and stand by us, and that we do it in a community. That is, we will belong to the church, and seek to serve Christ as Lord (one who holds authority over us) in connection with other Christians. Note, then, that Christ has opened the church to all ages, nations, and races. The church is not a closed community, open only to a select few. All are welcome in Christ's church. Part of serving him as Lord, part of putting our trust in his grace, is accepting all those who seek to belong to Christ, without putting up any barriers.

Then there is a question that the pastor asks of the whole church. This happens every time there is a baptism, or someone makes a public commitment, or profession of faith, as it is also called. Will you, the church, stand by this person, support them by your words and example, and help them grow in the Christian life? Making a commitment to Christ in The United Methodist Church is not a solitary adventure. It is a public commitment, to which the congregation responds with an answering commitment of its own. We are all in it together, and we take responsibility for each other's faith and life. Every time a baby is baptized, or a youth confirmed, or an adult makes a profession of faith, the whole church renews its commitment to the same causes and the same Lord.

Finally, the fourth question:

According to the grace given you, will you remain a faithful member of Christ's holy church and serve as Christ's representative in the world?

Faithful membership involves our prayers, presence, gifts, and service, as was pointed out in Section I. But it also involves serving as Christ's representative in the world. This is no casual question. It means that we will live our lives so that when people see us, they see something of Christ. We will represent Christ in the world. The truth is, sometimes we represent Christ very well. Other times, we do so poorly, and this leads outsiders to say such things as, "church members are hypocrites," or "if they just practiced what they say, I might take them more seriously." Either way, for good or ill, we represent Christ to the world.

The questions are not asked lightly. Nor should they be answered lightly. Taken together, they mean that you "bet your life" on the answers. There may be other gods in the universe—certainly there are secular "gods," such as wealth, power, and pleasure. But you choose to give your allegiance to Jesus Christ. You "bet your life" that he is the Way, the Truth, and the Life.

8

We're All In It Together

· ·

It was almost time. The event was the annual meeting of confirmation classes from churches across the conference with the Bishop. The Bishop stood up in the front of the sanctuary to begin the meeting. He was a tall, rather stern-looking man, dressed in a three piece suit and tie—in vivid contrast to the cut-offs and baggy pants of the junior high boys seated on the first row. Rather than make any kind of speech, the bishop left the chancel, walked down to the front pew and (with the microphone on) asked one of the boys seated there, "Young man, do you know why you are a part of the church?" The boy was already nervous about the bishop standing so close and the question just about put him over the edge. He turned pale, then flushed, and said quietly, "No, sir." (Good answer, when you haven't a clue what the correct answer is supposed to be.) "You're in the church because God called you to be," the bishop said in commanding tones, then turned around, went back to the chancel, and began the session. On the front pew he left a group of young boys who were totally goggle-eyed. God had called them?

So what does it mean to make a commitment to the church? Some Christian denominations operate on a "voluntary association" model. This means that people make a choice about whether or not to join the church. They join voluntarily, they can leave voluntarily, they can participate in the activities of the church, or not, just as they choose.

This is also the model on which civic clubs and similar organizations are built.

In practice, many United Methodists act as if we were also operating in a "voluntary association" model. But, as the story about the bishop and the confirmation class above shows, our official doctrine is far different. We believe that we are in the church because God called us to be. God doesn't call us dramatically, like St. Paul on the road to Damascus. Rather, God calls us in our baptism to be a part of the community of faith, the people of God, the church. When we make a commitment to Jesus Christ, as we saw above, we make some serious promises about how we will live our lives. And the congregation also makes, or reaffirms, some serious commitments as well. You see, we believe that we are all in it together. To be part of the church is to be part of a family, a community, to which many of us were committed when we were infants. Others of us make that commitment for ourselves as adults, when we become a part of the church for the first time.

As we have seen, in the service of baptism, confirmation, or other profession of faith, the congregation also makes a commitment. I used to tell my congregation that this was such a serious commitment I didn't want them to respond to the question unless they were willing to bet their lives on the community of faith. When I baptized my colleague's baby, I said to the congregation that what they were about to say was a promise that whatever he needed to live a Christian life as he grew up, they had already promised to provide. If he needed a Sunday School teacher when he was in third grade, it would not be a matter of asking if someone would. They had already promised that, back at this baptism. It would be a matter of saying, "It's your turn." I named a person in the congregation when I said that and, after the service, he came up to me and said, "I'd better go meet Ben, since I'm going to be his Sunday School teacher." That's the commitment we make as a part of the church.

The congregation promises some pretty radical things:

1. to proclaim the good news; i.e., to teach the faith,
2. to live following the example of Christ,
3. to surround the new Christian (of whatever age) with a community of love and forgiveness,
4. to help them grow in their trust in God,
5. to help them be faithful in their service to others, and
6. to pray for them, that they will be true disciples of Christ.

When we make a commitment to the church, we commit ourselves to that kind of community of love and service. We believe that we are all in it together, and that the faith life of every other Christian depends upon how we live and nurture them. I look back on my own life and remember all the faithful persons (including my parents) who taught me the faith in Sunday School; our church lay leader, whom we all wanted to be like when we grew up and who supported us and praised us for whatever we did; our youth leader, who taught us to pray; countless adults who gave us examples of service and outreach. Without them, would I (and my friends) have been the faithful Christians we are today? I doubt it.

You see, it's a challenge being a part of the church. We can't just go to worship and "hide." We make a commitment to be a full part of the community and live the kind of life that, if a child wants to be like us when she grows up, she'll be like Christ.

One other point. When we affirm the Apostles' Creed, or the Nicene Creed, we are sometimes troubled by the phrase, "one, holy, catholic, and apostolic church." We don't really know what that means, or, if we think we know, we don't like it. How, for example, can we say the church is one, when there are hundreds of denominations and sects, many of them absolutely sure they are the only true church? The oneness of the church comes, not from ourselves, but from Christ. Paul says, in his first letter to the Corinthian church, that because we partake of the same loaf, we are one. That unity is in our being rooted in Christ. The same is true about calling the church "holy." We all see examples of hypocrisy in church members who we know have done things the church abhors, and yet here they are. How can a church be holy with that kind of people in it? The truth is we're all sinners—that's right. But the holiness does not come from us. It comes from the holy God who calls us, who brings us salvation, who lives and works in the church day by day. Many Protestants don't like to say they believe in the "catholic" church, because they do not want to claim loyalty to the church of Rome. But catholic, in the creeds, means universal, the church of Christ spread throughout the world. And as for apostolic, we mean that the church is founded on the teaching and preaching of the apostles, who passed on what they heard Jesus say and saw Jesus do. This phrase has nothing to do with "apostolic succession," and everything to do with apostolic teaching and apostolic faith. With those understandings, we can affirm the creeds joyfully and honestly.

9

What Do United Methodists Believe?

● ●

"You can believe anything and be a Methodist."

"Methodists don't really believe in much except potlucks and fundraisers."

"One of the things I like about being a United Methodist is that I don't have to believe exactly like everyone else. I can think about my faith, be different, and still be a faithful member of the church."

"United Methodists are so broad-minded they're empty-headed."

Maybe you've heard some of those statements. Maybe you've even said them yourself. The truth is that United Methodists do have some core beliefs that we stress and that all of us are called to affirm. Those core beliefs are like the out-of-bounds line on a football field. They don't tell us what we can or can't think. They do tell us that there are boundaries. We can speculate all we want within the boundaries, but when we step out-of-bounds, we need to step back and re-think. The first set of boundary lines are the historic creeds. We know them as the Apostles' Creed and the Nicene Creed. Without getting bogged down in details (which is a whole other book), let's look at one example of how they function as boundaries. Early in the second paragraph of both creeds, there is the affirmation that Jesus is the Son of God. So here's how the boundaries function. We can speculate all we want about *how* Jesus is the Son of God. In fact, there are at least four or five different ideas about that in the New Testament. That's OK—it's within the boundaries. We only cross the boundaries and are out-of-bounds when we begin to question *that* Jesus is the Son of God.

With that example of boundaries before us, let's look at some teachings that United Methodists hold in common with all other Christians and then at some that are special emphases for United Methodists. The following brief statements are a kind of outline of the doctrines. Some of them we'll spend some extra time and space on.

BASIC CHRISTIAN AFFIRMATIONS[2]

God is Three-in-One—Father, Son, and Holy Spirit

One of the great mysteries of the faith is the relationship among the Father, Son, and Spirit. How can God be One and at the

2. All the material in this section is based on *The Book of Discipline of the United Methodist Church*. Nashville: The United Methodist Publishing House, 2000. p. 43-48

same time be Three? The question leads to all kinds of specula-
tion and analogies. The key is remembering the boundaries—so
long as we stay in the playing field, we can speculate all we
want. It's only when we deny that God is both One and Three
that we push the edges too far.

God is Creator

This is a given in Christian thought. The question is *how* God
creates. One answer, held by many faithful Christians, is that
God created the world by his Word, calling it into being in six
days. Another answer, also held by many faithful Christians, is
that God chose a long period of development and change to
bring about creation as we know it. Both answers play "in
bounds," affirming that God is the creator, but differing in how
God chose to create.

Human Beings Are Sinners, Who Need to be Saved

Remember that feeling, like you had lead in the bottom of your
stomach? You knew something was wrong, that relationships
were broken and needed to be mended. Worse, you knew that
you had to do something about the brokenness and the mend-
ing—and you hated the very thought of it. Remember? That's at
least one way of describing what we call sin. Sometimes the broken relationships are with other people, perhaps family
members or friends. Other times, we know the brokenness is in
our relationship with God. Some theologians say that second
brokenness is a primary sin which leads us to commit all kinds
of sins—you know, those things that are "against the rules," that
we do anyway. Oh, and one other thing. That feeling about the
lead in the bottom of your stomach? That may also be a form of
"prevenient grace" (see below, page 55).

We Are Saved through Jesus Christ

The key doctrine of Christian faith is that Jesus Christ is our Savior. The difference comes when we try to explain *how* Jesus saves us. Is it because of a sacrifice Christ made to the Father? Is it a victory over sin and death? Is it an example of love that leads us to love in return? All these, and more, have been held by faithful Christians throughout the centuries. But all agree on the key point—Jesus Christ is our Savior.

God Works in our Lives through the Holy Spirit, Both in Personal Experience and through the Church

We believe that God is not remote, somewhere off above the universe, but a God who continues to work in human life. Sometimes that is a direct work, in which the Spirit works directly upon an individual heart and mind. At other times, the Spirit works through the church, through preaching, teaching, the sacraments, and the example of other Christians.

We Are Part of Christ's Universal Church

When we say "catholic" church in the creeds, we mean the one, universal church that Christ called into being as his instrument for getting things done in the world. This statement also implies that all the diversity of Christian denominations are equally a part of that universal church, and that none of us has a "corner" on spiritual truth—no matter what we may think on our worst days.

We Believe that the Kingdom of God is Both Present and Future Reality.

We believe that the kingdom of God is the reign of justice, love, and righteousness, as God would have us live it. We believe that the kingdom was among us in the person of Jesus of Nazareth, and that we continue to live in the kingdom today. But the Kingdom has not yet come in its fullness. So we live both in the joy of knowing that the kingdom has come among us, and in the hope that it will come in its fullness. For many Christians, the coming of the kingdom in fullness is related to the Second Coming of Christ.

The Scriptures Are Authoritative in Matters of Faith

Christians believe in the Bible. Later in this section, we will take a more detailed look at how United Methodists believe that. Here, it is enough to say that all Christians give Scripture authority in questions of faith. Some Christians give the Scripture authority in all matters, including history and science; others do not.

We Are Justified by Grace Through Faith

Grace is the love of God poured out to us, love which we do not deserve (because of sin), and which we can never earn. Love describes who God is and how God relates to the world. It also describes the driving force behind our salvation. Justification comes from a Roman legal term which means, roughly, that we are guilty, but we are treated as if we are innocent. In Christian language, it means the same thing—that God freely takes away our sin and gives us new life. We gain the benefits of justification and grace through faith in what God has done in Jesus Christ. Another way to say this is that Justification means that God accepts us, just as we are.

All Christians Are Called to Ministries of Building up the Church, Reaching Out to the World, and Working for Justice

There was a sign on the church bulletin board: "Pastor, John Jones. Ministers: the entire congregation." We are all called to ministry. At one time we referred to that call as "the priesthood of all believers," but have found that phrase doesn't really say everything we want to say. "Ministry of all Christians" is a phrase that reminds us that each one is called to justice, outreach, compassion, and building up the church.

DISTINCTIVE WESLEYAN EMPHASES

These "distinctive emphases" have always been around in Christian thought, but they are particularly important to United Methodists—indeed, to all Wesleyans.

Prevenient Grace

Remember the lump of lead in your stomach? Remember we said that could be one form of prevenient grace? Here's what we meant. When United Methodists, following the example of John Wesley, talk about prevenient grace, we mean the form of God's love that always surrounds us, even before we have heard about it. It is God's grace that always surrounds us, which calls us to seek for God, and moves us toward repentance and faith. Sometimes, prevenient grace comes as "bad news," as a lump in the stomach, calling us to restore the brokenness in our relationships. And, sometimes, well, let's try another image. Have you ever been aware that there was an emptiness in your life, like a hole in your heart? That there was a place that needed to be filled with love and assurance and peace? That, too, is prevenient grace—God's love calling to us to turn to God to find the relationship that will fill up the emptiness, and plug the hole.

Justification and Assurance

We all know what a wonderful feeling it is to be with someone with whom we don't have to pretend, someone who accepts us just the way we are, warts and quirks and foibles and all. We can relax, we can be truly ourselves, we can find joy, because we are sure of the other person's love. That's the way it is with our relationship with God. Justification means that God accepts us just as we are, forgives our sins and restores us to relationship with God's self. This is also called conversion and new birth, when we get into the technical vocabulary of Christianity. Assurance means we can know that God has truly loved us and has saved us, instead of always wondering. Assurance means that we can relax in the presence of God and be truly ourselves. We know that God knows all about us and still loves us.

Sanctification (Perfection, Holiness)

Santification is God's continuing work in our lives, helping us grow in the knowledge and love of God and the love for our neighbor. This is perhaps the most significant Wesleyan gift to Christian doctrine. Not that the idea of holiness was a brand new one with Wesley. But it was Wesley who moved the concept from being reserved for a handful of people (monks in the early church, clergy in the modern church) and said that all God's people are called to be holy. In Sections III and IV, we'll explore a variety of ways in which holiness is lived out in the modern world.

Faith and Good Works.

We are saved by grace through faith, and not by how many good deeds we pile up. But knowing that God loves us and has saved us calls forth good works from us. Faith and works go together as part of a mature Christian life.

Mission and Service

These words remind us that holiness always involves love of neighbor, as well as love for God. It involves justice and the making of a better world for all God's children.

The Importance of the Church.

We are saved *from* sin; we are saved *to* a life of faith in the community of believers, the church. In earlier sections, we have talked about the importance of belonging, and the commitments we make to the church. Those commitments call for an answering commitment from the church, which means both individual persons and the total community. We are all in it together, and it is through our connection with other Christians that we are able to do the work of God in the world.

WHAT ABOUT BAPTISM?

United Methodists believe that baptism is a sacrament—a "means of grace," to use the technical vocabulary. "Means of grace" is a way of describing an avenue through which God's grace works in our lives, and becomes a reality. So there is something objective about baptism—God does something there. So what *does* happen in baptism?

In baptism, our ritual says,

> We are initiated into Christ's holy church.
> We are incorporated into God's mighty acts of salvation,
> and given new birth through water and the Spirit.
> All this is God's gift, offered to us without price.[3]

So what does all that mean? Baptism is a gift of grace. God gives us all that is promised in the first three parts of the paragraph. The first sentence is about belonging. We become a part of the church. In fact, United Methodists believe that one becomes a full member of the church in baptism, whether as an infant or as an adult. We become a full member of the family of God, just as a new baby becomes a full member of a

3. Baptismal Covent I, *The United Methodist Hymnal.* Nashville: The United Methodist Publishing House, 1989, p. 33

human family when he or she is born, not at some later time.
There is, to take the analogy further, always room for growth.
Children and youth have more responsibilities for family life
than tiny infants; so it is with church membership. But we
always belong. Belonging makes us part of the faith tradition.
We are "incorporated into God's mighty acts of salvation." We
become part of a heritage that is real in our lives. But, you
might protest, we weren't there when Moses led Israel out of
Egypt, or Jesus raised Lazarus from the dead. How can we
become a part of that? Think about your own heritage. We
weren't there when American troops froze at Valley Forge or
when George Washington signed the Constitution. We weren't
there when Pickett's charge broke against the Union cannon
fire at Gettysburg, or when Lincoln said, "Four score and seven
years ago. . . ." But we claim those moments for our own. They
are part of who we are, whether we were there or not. The same
is true in your family. You have stories and traditions that go
back for generations. You weren't there—but the stories help
shape who you are. The same is true for the church. That's why
we teach the faith, why it is important we know the stories and
pass them on to children. They make us who we are—and the
process begins in our baptism.

In baptism we are also given new life through water and the
Spirit. We don't know how that works. We *do* know that God
does something in us and for us in the act of baptism.

United Methodists don't insist on any one method of baptism. We normally use sprinkling, but we also do pouring and
total immersion. Each of these three ways has its own symbol-
ism and meaning. The important thing for the sacrament to be
done correctly is that we use water and baptize in the name of
the Father, Son, and Holy Spirit. We have a ritual, found in *The
United Methodist Hymnal*, that leads us through a rehearsal of

God's mighty acts of salvation, that calls for commitment from the person being baptized (or his or her sponsors), and from the congregation.

We do emphasize infant baptism, because we believe that baptism, among other things, is a sacrament of initiation. We initiate the child into God's family, and make him a member of the church.

United Methodists do not "christen." That is a naming ceremony, used in some denominations, but not recognized as baptism. For parents who want to postpone baptism so the child can make his or her own decision, we have a service of Thanksgiving for the Birth or Adoption of a Child. For all baptized persons, but particularly for infants, there comes a time when the church invites them to own the faith into which they were baptized. This we call confirmation.

WHAT ABOUT COMMUNION?

As you may have begun to suspect, United Methodists are different from many of our sister denominations in our beliefs and practices about Holy Communion (Lord's Supper, Eucharist) as well. We begin by understanding that Communion is a sacrament, a sign of God's grace and mercy for us. We live out the understanding of a sacrament by saying that no one is excluded from the Lord's table. You don't have to be a member of the United Methodist Church to take communion with us. In many congregations you will hear the pastor say something like, "Friends, this is a United Methodist service, but it is the Lord's table. All are welcome to share in the feast of love and joy."

So we practice what is called "open communion," meaning the sacrament is not closed to those who aren't members of the church. And (see What About Baptism, above), since we believe that children become full members of the church in baptism, we include children in the invitation as well. There is no minimum age that a person has to attain before he or she can receive the sacrament. In fact, I often said to my congregation that little children don't understand the sacrament, but they know it's a good thing, and they want to be a part of it. You can tell that by the size of the piece of bread they tear off the common loaf, and by the joy shining from their eyes as they participate in the sacrament.

We believe that the sacrament is a mystery, by definition something that we don't—and can't—understand. So, when adults tell me that children shouldn't be allowed to take communion (often because mine did, even at a very young age) because they don't understand it, I ask in return if they understand it, or should they be excluded as well. We know *that* God works in the sacrament, bringing love and mercy and peace to countless millions of people. We don't know *how* God works. But we rejoice because we know God does work.

John Wesley believed that Lord's Supper could be a means of conveying prevenient grace, justifying grace, and sanctifying grace. Those are all parts of the same grace, or love, of God, but each speaks to a different part of the faith journey. The sacrament conveys prevenient grace, because it speaks to the seeker of God's love and openness. For this reason, United Methodists continue to practice an open table. Wesley also believed that Lord's Supper could be a means of justifying grace. This is, you remember, the grace that saves us, that brings about conversion and new life. Many people have given their lives to Christ as they shared in the meal. And the sacrament conveys sanctifying grace to those who are in relationship with God and need to continue to grow. Whatever state of faith in which we might find ourselves, Christ meets us in the sacrament and gives us grace for our spiritual needs.

WHAT ABOUT THE BIBLE?

United Methodists, at our best, do not use the Bible as a weapon to bludgeon other people into believing what we want them to believe. We take the Bible very seriously, but we also read it as a very human document. Let's think about what that means. And to think carefully, we need to look at some technical vocabulary to see the part that the Bible plays in our faith.

"Do you believe that the Bible is the word of God?" Whenever I'm asked that question, it is often in a belligerent tone, as if I were doomed for all time if I said, "No." What I want to say is, "Yes, but I want you to listen carefully to what that means to me." (Usually, the person who asks that question in a belligerent tone doesn't want to listen carefully to me.) Believing that you are different, I'll say that the Bible is the *Word* of God, but not the *words* of God. That is, I believe, and I think United Methodists believe, that the Bible reveals the true Word of God, Jesus Christ. But not all the words in the Bible do that. For example, the Satan has some of the lines (see the temptations of Adam and Eve, Job, and Jesus). And not all the words about ceremonies in the Jewish Temple apply to Christian life today. But the *Word* is the person of Jesus Christ, who is the same yesterday, today, and forever.

But what about the inspiration of the Bible? Don't we believe that God inspired the Bible? The word "inspire" comes from the same root as the words for breathing. In fact, it means "to breathe into." Now, there are at least two major ways this can be interpreted. One way says that God put the words in the mouth of the writer(s) of the Bible and the words are there because God wanted them that way. Another way says that God's Spirit inspired the writer(s) so that they had keen insight into the ways of God and wrote about God's way with the world out of their own experiences. God inspired their thoughts, but not the exact words they used.

United Methodism says that the Bible "reveals the Word of God so far as it is necessary for our salvation".[4] This statement is important for what it does *not* say. It does not say that the Bible has all the truth about all topics for all time. Rather, it says the Bible has the word of God for all things necessary for salvation. Those things which are not necessary for salvation are in bounds, but we can speculate about them, question them, and even doubt them. We even disagree at times on which things are necessary for salvation. For example, is it necessary for salvation to believe that God created the world in six, twenty-four-hour days? Some Christians say "yes," some say "no." Both answers are "in bounds," as we understand the boundaries. The Articles of Religion of the Methodist Church say "whatsoever is not read therein, nor may be proved thereby, is not to be required of any man that it should be believed as an article of faith, or be thought requisite or necessary to salvation."[5] To many, that says that the Bible is a guide for our thought and action, but not all parts of the Bible are equally a guide. Wesley, for example, suggested that it was not necessary to try to follow all the laws for ritual worship in the Temple. That seems obvious, because the Temple in Jerusalem has not existed for nearly 2,000 years. Those teachings are clearly not on a par with the Sermon on the Mount, for example. Nor, he said, do we need to follow all the laws for the kings of Israel. However important they may have been for an earlier day, the context in which they made sense no longer exists.

4. The Confession of Faith of The Evangelical United Brethren Church, Article IV—The Holy Bible. Found in *The Book of Discipline 2000*. Nashville: The United Methodist Publishing House, 2000, p. 67
5. The Articles of Religion of The Methodist Church, Article V—Of the Sufficiency of the Holy Scriptures for Salvation. *The Book of Discipline, cit.* p.60

Finally, United Methodists think about their faith in different ways, but Scripture is always primary. We interpret Scripture and relate it to our lives through tradition, experience, and reason.

We affirm the Bible as the source of all that is necessary for salvation. When we read the Bible, we do so in the light of our own personal insight. We also are guided by the work of biblical scholars, men and women who have spent their lives trying to understand the meaning of the text in its original setting. This allows us to put ourselves in the place of those who wrote the Bible and experienced God in their day, so that we gain insight into what the Bible might say for our day.

We interpret Scripture in the light of tradition. We do not "re-invent the wheel" of understanding in every generation. There are thousands of faithful Christians whose lives reflect understandings of Scripture that shape us. These persons include great scholars such as Origen, Augustine, Luther, Wesley, and others. They also include our parents and grandparents and others in the faith communities in which we grew up. To be a United Methodist Christian in southern Indiana means coming out of a different tradition than a United Methodist in south India, or sub-Saharan Africa. Many cultures and traditions are represented in United Methodism, and those cultures and traditions shape how the Bible is understood in different parts of the world. There is something rich about hearing all the traditions. There is also tension and clashes of understanding when the traditions begin to talk to each other. The diversity of traditions reminds us that God's love is for all people, and we can learn to love, through the power of the Holy Spirit, those whose traditions are much different from ours.

We interpret Scripture in the light of experience, both our own personal experience and the experience of the church. A United Methodist group from Missouri goes to Mozambique for an

extended work camp/mission trip. They experience the poverty of
the people among whom they live, they learn something about
what it means to wonder where all the land mines are buried and if
it's safe to walk there, they see the tragedy of the orphaned children
that AIDS has left in its wake, and they experience the joy and love
of Mozambican Christians. They come home with a new understanding of the biblical message about caring for the poor, the
widows, and orphans. They will never again read the Bible in the
same way. Or, a group goes to visit the Holy Land as tourists. They
see the reality of the geography, they "walk where Jesus walked," and
they are never again able to read the Bible in the same way.

We interpret the Bible in the light of reason. At the most
basic level, this means asking ourselves, "Does my understanding of the Bible, my witness to its truth, make sense? Does it
hold together?" On a broader stage, we ask questions about
faith and science, for example. My experience with middle
school/junior high youth in confirmation is that one of the first
questions they ask if they are given the freedom is, "What about
God and evolution?" We try to understand how the findings of
biology, astronomy, geology, paleontology, and a dozen other
disciplines fit with our understandings of God as creator and
humanity created in the image of God.

All four, Scripture, tradition, experience, and reason, work
together in our minds and hearts as we try to make sense of the
world around us and to develop the most complete, most coher-
ent worldview that we can.

Section II Questions for Reflection

1. How do you understand your own commitment to Christ? To the church?
2. Do you see church membership as a voluntary association or as a call from God?
3. What does the language of the ritual for professing faith cause you to wonder?
4. As you read about doctrines that are distinctive to United Methodists, do you find those appealing to you? Why or why not?
5. Baptism has always been a key issue for United Methodists, and our predecessors, and it has been only in recent years that we have had an "official" theology about baptism and church membership. How do you see your own religious experience fitting with that understanding?
6. How do you understand Scripture? In what ways would you agree with the discussion of Scripture in this section? In what ways would you disagree?
7. Finally there is the issue of Christian perfection (sancti-

fication, holiness). Do you see "going on to perfection" as a realistic goal for your life and faith? Why or why not? What troubles you about the idea of perfection? What do you see as barriers to perfection in your life?

FOR FURTHER READING

Felton, Gayle C. *By Water and the Spirit: Making Connections for Identity and Ministry*. Nashville: Discipleship Resources, 1997. Contains the complete text of *By Water and the Spirit*, the understanding of baptism adopted by the 1996 General Conference, with comments and back-ground material to enrich understanding of the official document. Also contains a leader's guide for group study.

Jones, Scott J. *United Methodist Doctrine: The Extreme Center*. Nashville: Abingdon Press, 2002. A clear exposition of what United Methodists believe, and why.

Maas, Robin. *Crucified Love: The Practice of Christian Perfection*. Nashville: Abingdon Press, 1989. A careful study of what Christian perfection can mean for United Methodists (and others) in today's world. Includes a section of issues for the laity.

White, James F., *Sacraments as God's Self Giving*. Nashville: Abingdon Press, 1983. A helpful look at the sacraments of baptism and Holy Communion and their reality as a vehicle for God's grace.

Willimon, William H. *Remember Who You Are: Baptism—A Model for Christian Life*. Nashville: The Upper Room, 1980. A refreshing look at the meaning of baptism in the Christian life. Written before the adoption of *By Water and the Spirit*, it is still helpful in showing how baptism is determiner of Christian identity.

Section III

Growing

10

Sanctification

T he church council meeting had been going for two hours and the argument seemed to have no end in sight. (Yes, Virginia, arguments do occur in church council meetings!) The majority opinion agreed with the current speaker, who kept asking, "When are we going to stop growing? I don't know everyone anymore. We have added two more worship services and new Sunday School classes, and now you're starting to talk about building a new building. Wouldn't it be easier just to put a cap on growth?"

Putting aside for the moment the fact that many churches and their pastors would give their eye-teeth for a problem like this, what's wrong with that argument? Why shouldn't a church stay small and intimate and not have to worry about all the problems that come with growth? Here's a hint: "We grow or we die." Churches are like all other organizations. Either they keep moving ahead—growing, reaching out—or people begin to lose interest, drift off, and the organization slowly begins to die.

Oh, and the argument at the council meeting? It ended when one of the saints, who had not said a word all evening, stood up and quietly said, "We'll stop growing when we become the kind of church that none of us wants to belong to."

What is true of churches is also true of individuals. In our spiritual lives, we either grow or we begin to die, to lose the close connection with God and with others that gives us meaning and joy. Intellectually, we either grow or die. If we stop using our God-given gifts, whether those gifts are music, or language, or service, we also lose a great deal of identity and meaning in our lives. So what does it mean to keep growing in faith? How do we do that? The question about growth is what this section is all about. And, as followers of Wesley, we can't talk about growth without talking about sanctification.

Remember the earlier conversation about technical vocabularies? Sanctification is another one of those technical vocabulary terms that Christians use. It is also referred to as holiness or Christian perfection, and John Wesley firmly believed that his followers were called to "go on to perfection." This is the point where many of us begin to back up and say, "Whoa! There's no way I'm perfect or holy. Count me out." Many of us have memories of holiness as strict rule keeping. We had to be "holy" or we would never win God's favor—or a parent's favor, which might have been as important. Or we associate holiness with some Christian groups with holiness in their name and practices of worship that we considered really strange. Neither one of those is what Wesley meant when he talked about holiness (Christian perfection, sanctification). So what does that mean for Wesley's spiritual descendants? What does it mean that the bishop asks candidates for ordination as clergy if they are going on to perfection?

Earlier, when we talked about justification, we said it meant, among other things, that God accepts us just as we are. United Methodists believe that is true, in fact we "bet our lives" on it.

Sanctification, on the other hand, means that God accepts us just as we are, but doesn't leave us where we are. About the time we think we have our lives all worked out and another step taken, before we have a chance to even become comfortable with that, let alone complacent, God says to us, "That's good. Now, there's this other thing I've been meaning to talk to you about." That is, we are expected to continue to grow in our walk with God. That's where the language about sanctification (holiness, perfection) comes in.

Just as we need to know the technical vocabulary of our work world (whether that work is accounting, plumbing, computers, or whatever it may be) we need to have a sense about the technical vocabulary of our faith. So let's look at what sanctification is all about.

The Articles of Religion of The Methodist Church have this to say about sanctification:

> Sanctification is that renewal of our fallen nature by the Holy Ghost, received through faith in Jesus Christ, whose blood of atonement cleanseth from all sin; whereby we are not only delivered from the guilt of sin, but are washed from its pollution, saved from its power, and are enabled, through grace, to love God with all our hearts and to walk in his holy commandments blameless.[6]

That says a lot, and most of it in the technical vocabulary of theology. So let's look at the technical language and see what it means for our lives. Then we'll go back and look at some practical implications.

6. "Of Sanctification", The Articles of Religion of The Methodist Church, found in *The Book of Discipline 2004*. Nashville: The United Methodist Publishing House, 2004. p. 66

First, in order to understand the part about the fallen nature, you have to know that John Wesley believed in original sin, which means that we are all born sinners. That's difficult for most of us, who were raised on the idea that children are born good.

But the notion of original sin is part of our faith heritage and so we have to at least understand what it means. "Fallen nature" is a state of sin from which we are set free by the act of God in Jesus Christ. This is justification, which Wesley believed freed us from the guilt of sin. That is, we are guilty, but God treats us as though we were innocent and delivers us from that guilt. This is a great gift, and brings with it an equally great sense of relief.

The "blood of atonement" refers to the death of Christ on the cross, which acts as a perfect sacrifice for sin. We don't understand how this works and often feel uncomfortable or uneasy about the idea of blood sacrifice, or of Jesus dying as a sacrifice for our sins. Dealing with those ideas in any detail would need more space than we have here. So let's say that the idea of Jesus dying for our sins is an old, old idea in Christian thought. There are at least eight ways in which Christ's death (blood atonement) could work to free us from sin that are based in Scriptural understandings and are a part of the traditional teaching of the church. Each of them (like the blind men with the elephant) has a part of the truth, and all of them together don't have all of the truth. How Christ's death deals with sin is a great mystery. We can speculate on it, but we don't finally have a definitive answer. At the end of the search for understanding, we simply take it on faith that it does work.

After justification comes the process of sanctification. By God's grace we are not only freed from the guilt of sin, but also from the power of sin. That we can understand out of our own experience. How many times have you been tempted to do something for which you've just asked forgiveness? That is the power of sin at work. Sin is a pervasive reality in our lives, always trying to lure us away from God. The power of sin is not so much in the acts we commit, although those are important. The real power of sin is that we are tempted to believe we know better than God does what is good for our lives. That's very clear in the story of Adam, Eve, and the Snake, found in Genesis 3. There were three "good reasons" for eating the forbidden fruit— it was good to look at, it tasted good, and it would make whoever ate it like God, knowing the difference between good and evil. The story says that God had warned Adam and Eve not to eat it, because it would have dire consequences. But they thought they knew better, and tried to make their own wisdom the center of their lives, instead of God's wisdom. This is the primal sin, thinking we know better than God. In the process of sanctification, we are freed from the power that sin has over us in the temptation to think we know better than God.

You see, being sanctified, or holy, or perfect, doesn't necessarily mean we're better than other people. And it doesn't mean we never make mistakes. We can still add up a column of figures and get the wrong answer. Nor does it mean we don't sin. The aim is that we don't sin consciously and deliberately—but it is still possible to sin without intending to. We can hurt another person deeply by what seems to us an innocent remark. Or we start out to do good and the "law of unintended consequences" kicks in and we sin against a brother or sister. What being holy, or perfect, *does* mean is that sin no longer has power over us. We live in God and God's grace saves us from falling again into the power of sin. The Christian life is always a "going on to perfection," an awareness that we need to continue to grow in grace, in faith, in relationships with our neighbors, and in doing the works of God.

On the positive side, sanctification (holiness, Christian perfection) means that God's grace enables us to love God with all our hearts and to keep the commandments of love, justice, and mercy. Those are the key commandments on which all the other commandments are built.

Put it another way—the words for sanctification, holiness, and perfection in the language of the Bible mean something more like being complete, being all that we can be. They mean becoming who God intended us to become. The God-shaped hole in our hearts is filled and we begin to realize our potential. This doesn't necessarily mean that we realize our potential for music or sports or success in business. It does mean that we realize our potential as a human being and as a child of God. We can love freely, because we know God loves us. We can live life with zest because we know the One who is the source of life.

11

Don't Check Your Brains
At the Door

● ●

One of the standard plots in old western movies was the new marshal who came in to "clean up the town." One of the first things that marshal did was to post a notice that everyone who came into town had to check his guns while he was in town. Guns could be left with the marshal, or with the bartender in the saloon, but they had to be checked. No exceptions. When a person was ready to leave town again, he could get his weapons back. That law was intended to cut down on violence, particularly the kind that came from cowboys who had had too much to drink and weren't thinking clearly. It also disarmed the outlaw element and gave the marshal an "edge" when it came to the inevitable cinematic showdown. Sometimes the showdown came when the "bad guys" refused to check their guns and the marshal had to disarm them. OK, but what does that have to do with growing in faith?

There have been times in our history when the church required the faithful to "check their brains at the door" when they came to worship. The story of the church forcing Galileo to recant his findings that the earth revolved around the sun (and not vice-versa) is the most famous example of the "check your brains" mentality. But it is not the only one. Even in our supposedly enlightened day, there are all too many examples of congregations and denominations wanting to stifle thinking on the part of the people. For example, the controversy over stem cell research has led some churches to take a dogmatic stand on what they perceive as human cloning, or the destruction of human life, or both, and to refuse to even discuss the science behind the debate. Persons who disagree with that dogmatic stand are considered to be less than Christian, and sometimes even barred from the church. The same response often happens when issues such as abortion or the teaching of evolution in the public school come up. There is a strong anti-intellectual current passing as faith in our culture, telling people what they have to believe about current issues in politics, science, and public affairs. That is not to say that a Christian cannot have strong feelings about such actions and take action in the public arena. It *does* mean that Christians need to be aware of the best information that the sciences can provide before taking a dogmatic stand. It also means that no Christian has the right to impose his or her beliefs on another.

One of the glories of United Methodism and its predecessor bodies is that we have never, as a denomination, fallen into that trap. Oh, there have been times when we made public stands that turned out to be wrong. But we never denied our people the right to disagree and to try to change the public stand.

The Wesleyan movement began in a university setting, with the Holy Club. The members of the Holy Club were all Oxford students, and their "faculty advisor" was John Wesley. John himself was a part of the faculty of Lincoln College, Oxford. When the Holy Club met to study, they read the Scriptures and devotional books, but they also read the philosophers. John Wesley called himself *homo unius libri* (a man of one book—the Bible), but in truth he read widely. He was keenly interested in science, and was as fascinated by electricity (for example) as was Benjamin Franklin. He once interrupted a preaching trip to inspect the first iron bridge in England. Wesley edited and abridged a whole library of Christian books for his preachers to read. There was no anti-intellectualism in Wesley. He was curious about a wide range of issues and thought carefully about them. Sometimes he proposed solutions to social and economic problems that were unworkable at best, but he always thought carefully about what he was saying and doing.

American Methodism was (as were the United Brethren and Evangelical Association) a major supporter of learning. One of the tasks with which the circuit riders were charged by the conference was to sell books to their people. Methodists, United Brethren, and Evangelicals founded all sorts of colleges and seminaries (schools for young ladies) as they moved west. Their mission outreach to Native Americans and then to other peoples in other parts of the world always included schools and hospitals (using modern understandings of illness, health, sanitation, and clean water). Methodists, United Brethren, and Evangelicals responded in different ways to the scientific discoveries of the nineteenth century, particularly the theories of Charles Darwin. But they never took a stance that said, "This is the only way that our people can believe about this evolution theory," even when many may have wished they could. The followers of John Wesley have never had to check their brains at the door.

In practical terms, we still express that stance today. For example, I've taught a youth Sunday School class for years—in several different churches by now. I've always told those classes that the basic rule for being in the class was simple: "You can ask anything you want, about anything you want, at any time you want. And we'll deal with it. We may not deal with it at the time you ask it, but we will deal with it." That really came home to roost one Sunday, when, with five minutes to go in the session, a young lady asked, "Who wrote the Bible?" Two weeks later, we began a three-session study designed to give her information about her question. It's true that I have some advantages in training and background that many Sunday School teachers don't have, but all teachers and leaders can say, "I don't know, but we'll find out. Let's do it together."

On a denominational level, the same freedom exists. Only the General Conference can speak for the church, and General Conference doesn't say, "It's this way or the highway." Every decision of General Conference can be overturned by a future conference. The Social Principles, the collection of teachings on political, scientific, social, and other controversies of the day, are subject to change by the General Conference every four years. The voice of the church can be heard in the writing and adoption of the Social Principles, church law, theology, and all other issues. We don't check our brains at the door. One of the hot issues in the church today is the question of homosexuality, and the tangle of questions associated with it. As of now, the church has taken a position that says, in part, "homosexuals are persons of sacred worth" and "homosexuality is incompatible with the Christian life." The two statements don't seem to be compatible, which means that we, as a denomination, are conflicted about the issue, and the church continues to discuss and challenge current positions. Slowly we are struggling to bring together the traditions of the faith and understandings of Scripture in conversation with modern understandings of genetics and the experience of thousands of people who are "persons of sacred worth."

Part of the "don't check your brains at the door" issue is related to how United Methodists view the authority of Scripture, and what legitimate interpretations of the Scripture might prove to be. For persons who take a literal view of interpretation, the solution is pretty simple: if the Bible says it, it's true, and we don't have to think about it any more. Others say that the seven verses about homosexuality, for example, are outweighed by the overarching teaching about love and acceptance in the Bible, and that higher law of love is what must be obeyed. Obviously, those two (over-simplified) views of authority and interpretation lead to different views about exclusion/inclusion of persons in the church. United Methodists on both sides of the argument don't "check their brains," but put forth the best understandings possible of their positions. The discussion continues.

Wesley said that one of his goals was to "unite the two so long divided, knowledge and vital piety." United Methodists have always believed that it's possible to have both a strong faith and a grounding in academic disciplines. We not only don't have to check our brains at the door of the church, it's vital that we bring them in. Doubt is not the opposite of faith. Rather, doubt is an expression of faith. When we doubt we are thinking about who we are, what our relationship with God is, how we can believe what we are taught. That's a vital part of growing in faith.

Another vital part of growing in faith also involves using our brains. In a world that relies on sound bites and slogans, it's important that we have both a living faith and all the knowledge we can get our heads around. If we're going to take a position on, for example, stem cell research, we have to know a great deal about what stem cell research actually is and does. We also have to know a great deal about Scripture, our faith tradition, and how we can translate our faith into a meaningful position on ethical issues in today's world. We not only have to know the science, we have to be able to see God at work in the science. To take another example, the whole question of human evolution is still a live one in many parts of the world. Years of study of the science of evolution and study of the fossils (at least the pictures of the fossils) have led me to say that evolution is not only real, but that one can see God's creative handiwork in the process of evolution. Other honest Christians disagree with that position, and the conversation continues.

Why spend so much time talking about this topic? Because a part of growing in the Christian faith, of "going on to perfection," is dealing with the wealth of knowledge in all fields that is available to us. Another part of growing in faith is applying the insights from scientific, economic, and social knowledge to the ongoing conversation about how Christians should respond to the problems of the world as we try to help build the kingdom of God.

12

Spiritual Disciplines

• •

ere's what it comes down to: What are we willing to do in order to grow in faith and in love for God and neighbor? If we want to be the best we can be in anything, we have to work at it. Great musicians practice the piano, or violin, or whatever other instrument they play for hours at a time, trying not only to get the technical part (the notes, the tempo) correct, but also to be able to express the feeling in the music. Their practice needs to be as perfect as possible, so that their performance will also be as perfect as possible. Athletes also practice for hours on end. By August, the major league baseball season is moving into the final stages. The players still show up and take batting practice, fielding practice, and work on whatever they happen to be having trouble with at the moment. Football players study film by the hour as well as practice on the field. They want to know what their opponents do in certain situations, so they can be prepared. And they want to know that their teammates will be in a certain place on a certain play. They count on that, because they've practiced it so much. But they don't practice just to practice. Every practice move needs to be as perfect as possible so that it will also be perfect in the game. Simply going through the motions in practice and not worrying about getting things right is not enough. If we can't get it right in practice, we won't get it right in performance.

The spiritual life is no different. It requires diligent practice. There was a time in Jesus' ministry when he was called on to drive a demon out of a young boy. (See Mark 9:14-29) Judging from the description in the Bible, the boy probably had some form of epilepsy, but whatever people did not understand they called "demon possession." The boy's father complained that he had asked the disciples to cast out the demon, but they couldn't. So Jesus healed the boy. Later, the disciples asked: "Why couldn't we cast it out?" The answer was that particular kind of demon could be cast out only by prayer. The disciples hadn't been practicing their spiritual disciplines!

United Methodists, following the example of John Wesley, have certain routines we practice as part of our spiritual growth. They are called "acts of piety" and "acts of mercy." Acts of piety are those disciplines that help us grow in faith and love of God. Acts of mercy are those that help us grow in love of neighbor, lived out in our daily lives. A look at each of these suggests directions for our practice as well.

ACTS OF PIETY

These are usually defined as:

- public worship,
- the ministry of the word,
- the Lord's Supper,
- family and private prayer,
- studying the Scripture, and
- fasting or abstinence.

These were the practices recommended by John Wesley. In fact he did more than recommend—he *expected* that his followers would be involved in these practices.

In Section I, we talked about supporting the church by our presence. That is important, but presence is more than simply occupying space in a pew. It means to be actively involved in acts of worship with our Christian sisters and brothers, bringing all our senses, along with our minds, to bear on the worship of God. United Methodist Christians worship in different ways, from heavily traditional and liturgical to what is called "contemporary," with rock bands, videos, and extremely casual dress. The style of worship is not the key thing. We worship in whatever style we find comfortable and is a source for meeting our spiritual needs. The important thing is that no matter what the style of the worship service, that we are actively involved in it and engaged with it.

The ministry of the word can mean listening to Scripture read in worship, listening and taking in the sermon, and being involved in a Sunday School class or other form of Christian education that calls us to stretch our minds and hearts. This is the discipline that allows Scripture to speak to us through the interpretations of other people, whether the pastor or the writer of curriculum resources. The advantage of this discipline is that it opens the door to the full meaning of Scripture through the explanation of words or customs that we might not understand, because they come from a different culture. The lurking danger is that we take in whatever is said and assume it's true because the pastor said it. We also need to put our minds to work as we listen. United Methodists, you remember, interpret Scripture through tradition, reason, and experience. Engaging the spoken word means that we need to be asking questions. Does this fit the tradition of the church? Does it make sense? How does it fit with my experience? What is it calling me to do? What will the doing require of me? Is this a challenge to which I want to respond? Incidentally, asking those kinds of questions about the sermon is the highest compliment you can pay to the preacher—and a way to continue growing in faith.

Wesley was a strong believer in the spiritual power of the Lord's Supper (Holy Communion, Eucharist). He believed that his followers should share in the sacrament every time they came together. On the American frontier, that was not possible, because there were only a handful of ordained circuit riders, and they could not be present every time the little congregations met together. So American Methodists moved to the practice of Lord's Supper once a quarter. More recently, the church has moved to monthly celebrations of the sacrament. But what is there about this discipline that makes it important for our spiritual growth? John Wesley believed that the sacrament was both "converting" and "sanctifying." That is, persons who did not have a relationship with God in Jesus Christ could be brought into that relationship through participating in the sacrament. This is one reason United Methodists practice open communion. He also believed the sacrament helped Christians in their spiritual growth. There is something about the sacrament that draws us closer to God, gives us a spiritual depth that we did not have before, and draws us closer to each other in the church. And this happens whether we "feel" anything or not.

Prayer seems to be so obvious as a spiritual discipline. But what seems to be obvious is not always practiced. If we had a friend about whom we cared a great deal, we would call, email, write, whatever form of communication it took to keep that relationship alive. If we did not, the friendship would wither away for lack of nourishment. That's how it is in our relationship with God, as well. If we never take time to talk with God (pray) we soon find that the relationship begins to wither away from neglect. We need to set time aside each day for conversation with God, both telling God our needs and hopes, and listening for what God might say to us. It is also important to pray as a family. This part of the discipline might be a little more formal, in that printed prayers and other devotional material might be used. The discipline is important for adults as a part of their own growth. It is also important as an example to children in the home and as a foundation for their own growth and faith. The United Methodist Church, through The General Board of Discipleship, makes a variety of resources available for prayer and reflection, as well as for reflection and practice in other "acts of piety." They include *The Upper Room, The Upper Room Disciplines, A Disciple's Journal, Alive Now,* and *Devo'Zine* (for teens), as well as a wide range of books on prayer and other disciplines. For anyone struggling to seriously begin a practice of prayer, these resources would be valuable indeed.

Searching the Scriptures meant for Wesley the personal study of the Bible, in addition to what one hears at church. Some Christians study the Bible on a systematic basis, such as reading it through from beginning to end, or reading faithfully the lectionary passages for each week. Others read more at random, either searching for specific guidance, or choosing to read books of the Bible at random. No one way is necessarily better than another. The key is that one studies the Scripture. Nor do we check our brains at the door when we study. We continually ask questions. What is this text saying? Does the history behind the text make a difference to the way I understand it? What kind of literature is this? (We read poetry differently from the way we read narrative, for example.) What metaphors or other images make the passage more immediate? What does the text want me to do? Am I willing to do it? A key part of this discipline could become the use of commentaries or Bible handbooks as a part of our Bible study. The background material broadens our horizons about another culture. The reflections on the Scripture (in commentaries) help us think about the implications of what we've read and sharpens the way we ask questions.

Fasting or abstinence was an important discipline for John Wesley, and it continues to be important for Christians today. For example, the bishops of the church commit to fast once a week in solidarity with the hungry of the world. In today's America, with its obsession with body image and thinness often leading to bulimia or anorexia or other potentially harmful practices, fasting is not always recommended. When it is practiced, however, it needs to be a spiritual discipline, and not a ploy to lose weight. We need to know *why* we are fasting, *how* we will safeguard our health, *what* difference we expect the fast to make in our lives. Do we, for example, fast and use the money normally spent on food to provide assistance to people who are truly hungry? Do we fast as a way to discipline our bodies so they become servants of the spiritual life? Abstinence is a safer practice to recommend in today's world. It is a giving up of certain foods and practices for a higher good. We abstain from alcohol, for example, because we are aware of the potential dangers in alcoholism. Some of us abstain from fat, or sodium, for the sake of our health. We give up something we enjoy for the sake of the higher good of a healthy body, one that enable us to live longer and enjoy life with zest.

ACTS OF MERCY

When, through participation in acts of piety, we come to love God more, we are inevitably drawn to acts of mercy, to doing good to our neighbors. John Wesley urged his followers to do good to all persons, as fully and completely as we can. Doing good included specific acts, such as

- feeding the hungry,
- clothing the naked,
- visiting the sick and prisoners,
- caring for the sick, and
- educating the illiterate.

He also encouraged his followers to do business with each other, if possible, to hire each other when extra employees were needed. This was not an act of exclusion, but an act of mutual support in the community of faith. We can't live a life of economic isolation, doing business only with those like us. But we need to be aware of others in the congregation who have economic needs, and to work to meet those needs whenever possible. Many United Methodists have found fulfilling jobs because of the network of acquaintances within the church.

United Methodists have always been involved in acts of mercy, from the days of the Holy Club until today. In your local church, you may have a food pantry, or cook and serve meals to the hungry once a week or more. You may have a thrift store where good used clothing can be purchased at minimal prices. Almost every congregation makes a special effort to provide food, clothing, toys, and other necessities at Thanksgiving and/or Christmas. Many churches have intentional "prison ministries," either at a state or federal prison, or a county jail. These ministries are often ministries of presence, but they may include Bible studies, educational groups to help persons earn a GED, work with the families of those who are incarcerated, and so on. We visit the sick in hospitals and at home. Churches are often involved in literacy programs to some degree. All of these can take place in one's local community, through our direct efforts, or half-way around the world, through our giving to ministries of the general church. Those are great gifts that the church offers to the world, and we need to be constantly aware of the opportunities to do good that come our way.

ACTS OF JUSTICE

Today, however, there is a need to go deeper than simple acts of mercy. There is a need for "acts of justice" as well. In the Old Testament, justice is most often defined as being sure that persons have what they need in order to live a fulfilling life. That doesn't mean plasma TVs, but the basics of food, clothing, shelter, education, and health care.

So we may ask ourselves, "It's good that we feed the hungry once a week at church, but what's wrong with our society that people are that hungry in the first place?" "Why are there so many people without health care and/or health insurance?" Is there a flaw in the medical system that needs to be addressed? What does public policy do about health care costs? When we begin to ask questions like those, we inevitably come to the question, "What do you expect me to do about it? The problem is so big, and I'm one person. What difference can I make?" The truth is, you may not make much difference as an individual (though you may). But working with others through the church gives you a large group to tackle issues. Remember that the church working together under the leadership of persons like Dr. Martin Luther King, Jr., changed American life by doing away with segregation in schools, public facilities, public transportation, and ensuring that all citizens had equal access to the voting booth.

We, too, can make a difference. The church, working together, could challenge economic and social systems that leave some people out of the economic banquet. Why do people go hungry in the wealthiest society in human history? Why is it that some people who work hard, maybe holding down three or more jobs as a family, can't afford health care for their children? Is that a systemic problem, one that needs to be addressed by the entire body politic (all of us)? If it is, what can one person, or one group within the church do about it?

13

A Model for Growing

Where do we find the enthusiasm and the strength for living out all those acts of mercy and acts of justice? We find them in two arenas. First, we find them in our spiritual disciplines, our walk with God. Second, we find them in relationships. One of the strengths of the organized church is that it provides for us a community of like-minded people who bear us up and help us move on in our walk with God and our service to others. For example, Kate works in her church's kitchen each week, preparing and serving meals to persons who are hungry. Part of the challenge of that task is to sit down and eat with the guests, talk with them, hear their stories, come to know them as people. At a recent meeting of the church council Kate said, "I'm so grateful for the opportunity to serve those meals. I've wanted to do something for others, but didn't know how. The church has given me that chance and given me friends who work with me and help me be more open to people in need. Thank you."

What happened in Kate's life? She worked with Sally, who was so much at ease mingling with the guests and hearing all about their lives. One Saturday, Sally came back to the kitchen and said, "Kate, you've got to hear this. There is a lady here who has read all the Oz books." Now Kate didn't know anything about Oz except the movie with Judy Garland, but she soon found out! The people in the church helped her be outside herself and reach out to others.

We also gain strength and vision from our relationship with God, and our understanding, however faint, of the Trinity. The essential nature of the Trinity is relationship. That's why we talk about Father, Son, and Holy Spirit, rather than some other terms such as Creator, Redeemer, Sustainer. The latter are true, but they describe the functions of each of the persons of the Trinity. The traditional language, however exclusive and outmoded it might seem to some, focuses on relationships. In relationship the persons of the Trinity share love with each other. This sharing leads to an overflow of love which led to the creation of the world, the salvation brought about in the life, death and resurrection of Jesus Christ, and the power of the Holy Spirit present in the church.

Now, what does that have to do with us and our growth in faith? From reflecting on the Trinity, we learn about relationships. We learn that the key to relationship is loving and sharing. We learn that the persons of the Trinity support each other, so that whatever function we talk about, all three persons are involved. That's true of creation; it's true of the Son becoming flesh, living among us, and dying for our sin; and it's true of the work of the Spirit through the church. As we grow in faith and understanding, we begin to reflect in our own lives the model we see in the Trinity. We live out relationships of support and accountability. We share love among ourselves, which results in an overflow of love to others. We share ourselves with others, and discover new power and richness in the sharing.

Section III Questions for Reflection

1. Do you feel more comfortable now with the idea of sanctification? What specific insights helped you feel more comfortable?

2. Challenge yourself to commit to specific acts of piety. For the next two months, for example, commit to attending worship regularly. Or, if you already do that, commit to regular Bible study and prayer. Set aside time each day for that. Write that time into your planner, so that you have an appointment you have to keep.

3. Make a similar commitment to one act of mercy. Find out ways you could help others through your church. Volunteer to help one day a week, or one day a month, for the next two months. At the end of that time, stop and reflect on what the experience has meant for you. Consider what you will do the following two months.

4. Acts of justice are much harder for most of us than acts of piety and acts of mercy. In what acts of justice is your church, or individuals (groups) within the church

involved? Are those issues in which you have an interest? Find out more about the issues and ways you could become involved to make a difference.

5. Do you check your brains at the door when you go to worship? Does the church expect you to check your brains? Be alert to the way Scripture and tradition are presented in worship and/or educational ministries. How are the results of study in the sciences presented? Are you encouraged to raise questions? Why or why not? If you are encouraged to ask questions, express your thanks for that gift. If you are not, ask, "Why not?"

FOR FURTHER READING

Gooch, John O. *John Wesley for the 21st Century*. Nashville: Discipleship Resources, 2006. A look at Wesley's thought on a variety of topics, in dialogue with today's world. A helpful feature of the book is suggestions for how Wesley's thought and practice could become models for our faith and action.

Jones, Scott J. *United Methodist Doctrine: The Extreme Center*. Nashville: Abingdon Press, 2002. Jones deals with United Methodist doctrine in a way that makes it readily available to and useful for us today. He covers in more detail several topics that are dealt with in this section.

Yrigoyen, Jr., Charles. *John Wesley: Holiness of Heart and Life*. Nashville: Abingdon Press, 1996. An excellent source for Wesley's thought and its relevance for today. A chapter dealing with spiritual formation in the Wesleyan tradition is particularly useful with this section.

Section IV

Living

14

It Isn't Easy Being a Christian!

• •

It isn't easy being a Christian! It takes time and diligence. For example, it takes time to sort materials for recycling. If there is no curbside recycling, it takes time and effort to get materials to the recycling center. It would be so much easier just to throw it all in the trash. But at least most Christians believe that God has gifted us with stewardship over the world. That stewardship includes caring for the environment and not being wasteful of resources, among other things. So our faith leads us to specific actions, such as recycling. It's one small way we live out our faith in caring for the world, and for future generations.

Driving is another example. Most drivers in the United States seem to treat the speed limit as a suggested minimum. They weave in and out of traffic at high speeds, all the while juggling coffee, cell phones, and any number of other things that distract their attention from their driving. This is not to say that staying within the speed limit will make you a Christian. It won't. But, in addition to the legal issues about speeding, there are also some other points to consider. One is the wear and tear on nerves—your own and those of the drivers around you. Another is the question of gasoline usage and the dwindling petroleum resources of our planet. Beyond "keeping the commandment" of the legal limit, there are issues of conservation, safety, and concern for others. In fact, one might say that keeping a reasonable speed is a way of loving your neighbor.

Not that loving your neighbor is as easy as we sometimes make it sound, either. After all, our neighbors, whether those next door or across the street, or those we meet in church, in business, at social events, are not always congenial people. They get on our nerves. They have different understandings about all kinds of things—religion, politics, economics, and a host of other issues. It's not easy loving them all the time.

In this section, we'll be talking about how one lives as a Christian—personal ethics and morality; social ethics, also called social holiness; and where the church belongs in the world. Finally, we'll look at the Social Principles of The United Methodist Church as a guide for faithful living in a complex and often confusing world.

15

Personal Ethics and Morality

● ●

Tom belonged to a service club, and lived out what he considered to be the principles of the club. He worked at the club's service projects, showing up early and leaving late, always cheerful and helpful. He worked at the fundraisers the club put on, and personally donated money to the club's charitable foundation, which was used for good works. On top of all that, Tom was a big tease, and usually had people around him laughing and sharing his joy in life. But he didn't think he was doing anything out of the ordinary. Imagine his surprise one day when one of the other members of the club said to him, "I've always thought of you as being what a Christian should be. You're my model and when I think about doing something, I always ask myself if this is what a Christian like Tom would do."

What was there about Tom that made this other club member say something like that? On the surface, you couldn't tell Tom was a committed Christian. He didn't wear a cross or a WWJD (What Would Jesus Do?) bracelet. He didn't go around talking about his faith. But his faith shone through who he was and what he did, so that others saw it in him. St. Paul once said to the Corinthian church that they were Christ's letter of recommendation. That's what Tom was for his friend.

So Tom's personal life represented Christ to his friend. Is that what personal morality is all about? Isn't morality supposed to be about keeping the rules and doing the commandments? What are the rules? Ah, that's a good way to phrase the question. John Wesley wrote for his followers what he called the General Rules of the United Societies. He laid down three rules. First, don't do any harm; avoid evil. Then he gave a list of examples that applied directly to his day. They included such things as working on the Lord's day, drunkenness; slaveholding, buying smuggled goods, charging exorbitant interest, wearing gold or expensive clothes, self-indulgence, borrowing without intending to repay, taking things on credit. Some of the items on that list may seem to no longer apply. No one holds slaves anymore, obviously, at least not in the United States. But many people hire illegal immigrants and pay them "slave wages" under the threat of exposing them as illegal if they complain. And any economist will tell you that buying things on credit puts many U.S. citizens in economic jeopardy! Those are just two examples of "the more things change, the more they stay the same." Given that cliché contains some truth, can we learn from Wesley and other parts of our tradition about how to live in our day?

Wesley's second rule was to do good. Again, Wesley had a list of examples of what he considered to be good actions. And, again, some of them might not seem relevant today. But doing good is always relevant, and we can think of examples that would fit our situations. In fact, re-writing Wesley's list so that it fits today is an interesting exercise in how we define morality.

And the third rule? It was to "attend upon all the ordinances of God." That doesn't need to be rewritten to fit our world. By it,

Wesley meant that Christians should be attentive to public worship, prayer, Scripture study, and the other spiritual disciplines that we discussed in Section III, Growing. The important thing to remember is that refraining from evil and doing good are not just things we easily will to do. They are disciplines in themselves, and depend on a solid foundation in the spiritual life to provide guidance and strength for doing the right thing.

But how do I know what is the right thing? Personal moral decisions aren't always clear-cut. There are nuances and consequences, even unintended consequences, to our actions. How can we know what is the right thing to do?

There aren't, as the question indicates, clear answers for every moral decision. Oh, there are for some decisions, but not all. There are, however, some sources for helping us determine personal morality that are available for all of us. Using those sources means we have to engage our brains and think carefully about what we're doing. They are helps, but not final answers.

Obviously, the most important source is the Scripture. How we use Scripture as a moral guide is the key. We have to do more than proof-text, which consists of pulling out a verse here and a verse there to support what we really want to do. We have to look at the broad guidance of the Scripture on issues and not just pick our pet verses. We've already seen, for example, how many times the Scripture admonishes God's people to care for the needy, the weak, the oppressed, and the alien. That carries a greater weight than Paul's single statement to the effect that the church should not feed people who sit down and wait for Jesus' return and not work. We also have to look at the context of verses that we pull out of Scripture. Paul's statement is one good example. Taken in its specific context, it doesn't mean to neglect all people who aren't working, but do expect some accountability and responsibility for those who refuse to work because they believe Jesus is returning soon. Or take Jesus' statement that you always have the poor with you, which is often used to "prove" we don't have to worry about the poor. In context, the rest of the verse says that you can care for the poor whenever you want to, the very opposite of what it is often misused to mean. When we use the Scripture carefully and thoughtfully, however, it is the single greatest resource we have for personal morality and ethical decision-making.

The Scripture also leads us to consider the bracelet question—WWJD? What would Jesus do in any given situation? To have any idea at all how to answer that, we have to know Jesus and his teachings. What do the Gospels say Jesus did? How did he act? Take the simple question of judging other people—Jesus clearly said not to judge, but we do it all the time. What would Jesus have us do about caring for others? His own life seems to say that Jesus was concerned we show care for all, including our enemies. If we are going to use the question, "What would Jesus do?" as a moral guide, we have to be grounded in what Jesus did and said. Again, the moral and ethical issues that we face force us back to spiritual disciplines, in this case the basic one of carefully reading our Bibles.

Another source of ethical decision-making is the tradition/heritage of the church, both the whole span of the history of the church, and the particular traditions of The United Methodist Church and its predecessors. The Wesleyan emphasis on holy living and sanctification is a solid foundation for moral decision-making, whether we're talking about personal honesty or feeding the hungry. If we take seriously the call to be holy, to be as the Scripture says, "perfect as your Father in heaven is perfect" (Matthew 5:48), we remember that our model for the moral life is Jesus Christ and the commandment of love. Susan was having a terrible time getting along with another person in her Sunday School class. The other person was a complainer, and always criticized other people, including the pastor, for the way they lived their lives. Susan talked to the pastor about it, and confessed that she was beginning to detest the other person. She knew that was wrong, but she didn't seem to be able to help it. The pastor said, "I understand what you're saying, and the person is clearly disruptive. But remember, she is one of those for whom Christ died." Susan wasn't sure that was an answer, but the more she thought about it, the more she realized her attitude toward the person was changing. She still was aware of the person's faults, but was able to see beyond the faults to a person who was lonely and hurting. Susan began reaching out to the other person and tried to help her find the love God had for her. There was no instant miracle, and the person is still a complainer, but Susan is convinced she made the right moral choice. Incidentally, Susan is a far better person because of what she did and who she became in the doing.

A third source for personal morality is our native reason. One way in which reason helps make moral decisions is that it helps us identify what the real issues are. Exactly what is it that you are being asked to do? How does that action affect your sense of self-worth (if you do this, will you be able to look in the mirror tomorrow?) What will be the consequences if you choose to do what you're asked? Consequences for you? For other people? Which consequences are you most able to live with? (recognizing that there are very few perfect choices).

A fourth source would be your own personal tradition. What values do you and your family traditionally stand for? As in, "a (your name here) doesn't do that"? Our parents and grandparents often saw to it that the family name stood for something. Their values, outmoded though they may seem on the surface, can be a valuable help in developing your own personal morality. Who am I? What do I stand for? What are my values? And what in this choice best reflects my values?

Of course, in our rapidly changing world, we face moral decisions that our ancestors never dreamed of. Jim was involved in a head-on collision that left him paralyzed below the neck. He would never be able to move again, or to breathe without assistance from a machine. Of course, some people have recovered in such situations and led fairly normal lives. But Jim had always insisted that quality of life was as important as length of life, and said he didn't want to be kept alive by machines. He had also suffered some brain damage in the accident, and could not communicate with his family. One doctor suggested that he was technically brain dead and that the family needed to think about what to do. That meant, did they remove Jim from the machines and let him go in relative peace? Or did they try to keep him alive with almost no quality of life? If that were a member of your family (and it might very well have been) what decision would you make? How would your sources of personal morality help you in the decision?

That's a decision that, so far as we know, Jesus never had to make, so we can't rely on a simple going back and doing what Jesus did. But what is there about who Jesus was and the principles by which Jesus lived his life, that could help us in a situation like that?

Tackling Some Issues Head-On

What about some of the big issues? I go to church and hear the preacher say that abortion is a sin. My sister had an abortion. Is she a sinner? What does God think about her? That question reminds us, once again, that faith and reason belong together. If we are faithful Christians, if we want to make a difference in the world, if we want to have a true moral voice, we need to know what we're talking about. Christians honestly disagree about the morality of abortion, for example. But the issue goes much deeper than the morality of a clinical procedure, important though that may be. The act of abortion is only the tip of the moral iceberg, the part we see. The real question is not the medical/surgical act, although it is clearly important. The real question is, "When does life begin?" Christians need to read and study and pray thoughtfully about that question, because it is what makes all the difference in the debate. The abortion issue is only one of dozens of ethical questions that face us on a daily basis. The question about the beginning of life surfaces again in the debates on stem cell research. An honest moral decision has to go deeper than rhetoric and ideology. There is plenty of that around, on both sides of any decision. The point here is that we have to use our brains in dealing with moral issues. And why? Because most moral issues are so complex that simple answers will not work. Questions such as these affect the church as an institution and who we are in the political realm as well. Many states have held or are holding referenda on stem-cell research, and some churches are fully involved in the political debate. As a member of the church—whether your congregation is politically involved or not—and as a citizen, you face the responsibility of choice. Do you agree with your church's position enough to support it publicly in the political realm? When you enter the voting booth, how informed will your vote be by both science and faith and their teachings on the question? Personal morality also has consequences for public life.

What do we do in those situations where a supervisor or manager asks us to do something that we feel is wrong? Where do the demands of the job threaten our values?

Not easy questions. We could wish that we would always say, "That's wrong and I can't do it," but we know there are serious consequences to that kind of stand. Our jobs may be at stake. Which could mean our children wouldn't be able to have the dental work done they need. Our family would not have health insurance, swimming and ballet lessons would go by the wayside, family life would be disrupted. How do you weigh all that against the manager's demands? How wrong are the demands? Those are not easy questions, which reminds us, once again, that personal morality is not always clear-cut.

When Jesus called us to love our neighbor, he was not talking about some kind of tender feeling toward people we know. He was talking about messy moral choices, dealing with people we sometimes don't even like, and still wanting the very best for them. An adult Sunday School class spent the morning talking about how to relate to panhandlers on the city streets. Should they give them money? Food? What to do? No one wanted to help support a drug or alcohol habit, though one person argued that our responsibility was to offer help, and give the recipient the freedom to do whatever they wished with the help. So was it a better solution to take the person to a restaurant and buy them a meal? Do you see all the moral issues there? At the end of the discussion, there was an emerging consensus that the important thing was to humanize panhandlers, stop and talk, get to know them by name, and then decide what to do about physical help. What we do about panhandlers is, in fact, a moral choice.

Loving our neighbor (the second great commandment) often leads us into issues bigger than just personal morality. But the choice always begin in a personal moral dilemma.

17

Social Ethics and Social Holiness

●●●

Behind the question about how to deal with panhandlers, there is a deeper question about people in our society who are hungry. United Methodists, from the time of Wesley, have been concerned about poverty and hunger and disease. Epworth United Methodist Church, located in a neighborhood where many residents are always on the edge of homelessness and despair, serves a hot meal twice a week to persons who are hungry. They also operate a food pantry that provides staple food items to families who face more month than paycheck, and cannot feed their children in a given week. St. Andrews United Methodist Church is located in an affluent suburb of the city where Epworth is also located. St. Andrews does not have hungry people in its neighborhood, but its members regularly bring staple food items to the church for delivery to Epworth's pantry. Both are dealing with the problem of hunger in their city. John Wesley, who often said that there is no holiness except social holiness, would applaud their efforts.

United Methodists also raise the question, "What is wrong with the economic and social systems of the wealthiest country in human history, that we have large numbers of people who are hungry—and not by choice?" Today, we are asking the same question about health care. What's wrong with the systems that we have so many people who are uninsured? So many have inadequate health care, which in turn affects learning, work, and family wellbeing? Why are there so many people whose only health care is the emergency room, the most expensive care in the entire health-care system, and an expense that many hospitals wind up eating? The same kinds of questions could be asked about housing, about educational systems that regularly turn out young adults who are functionally illiterate, about safety, about the environment.

None of those questions is easy to answer. Trying to think about solutions is enough to give us a major headache. Even the act of raising the questions sometimes brings down public wrath on the heads of the people asking them. And yet raising the questions is part of the calling of Christians. John Wesley called that "social holiness." By that phrase I think he meant that it's not enough for a Methodist (as they were called in his day) to have a personal relationship with God in Jesus Christ. Our relationship with God must show itself in acts of mercy— and acts of justice. Wesley was more than willing to work to change the economic and social systems of his day in order to help those in need. He wanted to tax the horses of the wealthy, for example, so that the wealthy wouldn't keep as many horses and the grain previously fed to horses could be freed up for the use of the poor. He also wanted to do away with breweries, partly because alcoholism was such a problem in his day, but mostly because the breweries used so much grain that was no longer available to make bread for the poor. Because he believed so strongly in responsibility and accountability, Wesley did not want to simply give the bread to the poor. He thought that was demeaning. Instead, he wanted bread to be plentiful, so that prices would drop and the poor could afford to buy it. He thought that was both merciful and just.

What is justice? In its most basic form, justice is seeing that everyone in a society has his/her basic needs met. Those basic needs include food, clothing, shelter, health care, and education. United Methodists base their faith on Scripture first of all, remember? The Scriptures are full of admonitions about caring for the poor, for the most vulnerable members of society, those who for whatever reason cannot care for themselves. In the Old Testament, the worthiness of the king was judged on how well he did that. The Psalms and the Prophets are full of admonitions about caring for the poor, seeing that they have justice. Amos, for example, railed against an economic system that, as he put it, "[sold] the righteous for silver and the needy for a pair of sandals." (Amos 2:6b) His argument was against the system of selling free men into slavery because they could not pay trifling debts. That's not just an ancient thing, either. Wesley's father was put into prison at least twice for debt. The system was structured such that if you couldn't pay your debts, you were put in prison until you could. Of course, while you were in prison, you couldn't earn any money with which to pay your debt, which made the whole system self-defeating. But, hey, no one ever said that public policy always makes sense! Another Old Testament example that speaks directly to the heart of a major contemporary debate: there is one time where the Old Testament says "love your neighbor" and dozens, perhaps hundreds, where it says to work for the welfare of the aliens among the people of Israel. In sum, the high social morality of the Old Testament was "who are the weakest and most vulnerable in our society? Who are those who cannot, for whatever reason, make it under our system? It is our responsibility to see they have what they need in order to be a fully functioning part of society." That's social holiness at its finest and clearest.

The kingdom of God that Jesus preached was a radical (getting at the root of) teaching about justice, as well. Take two examples. The well-known parable of the Good Samaritan is one we read and feel good about. What a great example of how to care for an innocent victim, we think. And look—it was the Samaritan, the person that society turns its back on, who helped. At various times in U.S. history, the equivalent of the Samaritan would have been the native American, the African-American, the Irish immigrant, the gay man, the illegal migrant worker. That's one possible lesson about social holiness we could gain from that parable. But there is also at least one other possibility. What if, every time the Samaritan made that trip from Jerusalem to Jericho (and let's assume he was a business man who made the trip regularly) he had to stop and tend to somebody's injuries and get them to the emergency room? He pretty soon would have been in the office of the Roman official in charge of police activity, wanting more protection for travelers on that road. He would have wanted a change in the system so that people could be safe.

The other example about the kingdom of God is the story about the rich man who wanted to know what he had to do to enter the kingdom. Jesus told him to follow all the conventional morality; i.e., the Ten Commandments. When the man said he had done all that (he was good on personal morality), Jesus said he lacked only one thing. To enter the kingdom he had to sell everything he owned, give it to the poor, and come follow Jesus.

The kingdom is about, among other things, distributive justice. There is plenty of wealth, food, shelter, education, health care, and so on, to go around. The problem is that not everyone has equal access to that wealth. To raise the question about social and economic systems in our time is to be faithful followers of Scripture.

18

Where Does the Church Belong?

> "" The church has no business getting involved
> in politics. ""

That's the cry that arises every time there is an election, or a pastor raises moral questions about a political issue. The truth is we are involved in politics all the time. Church people vote. They campaign for candidates and for or against issues. In the United States, we have a long tradition of separation of church and state, by which we mean 1) the state cannot establish a religion; that is, make one denomination or faith tradition the official religion of the nation; and 2) the church cannot dictate to the state how it should act. That is an important principle in our tradition, and one well worth preserving and cherishing.

Having said that, the church *does* have a role in national life. Based on the scriptural precedents of the Prophets, the church is called to be the conscience of the nation. We have the right, indeed the duty, to speak up for honesty, truth, morality, and the just treatment of minorities and persons who are marginalized. That does not mean we have the right to impose a particular morality upon the nation. It does mean that the church raises moral issues and calls the political, economic, and social systems to accountability for their actions. This call for accountability is behind the story of Jesus driving the money changers out of the Temple. Both they and the sellers of animals for sacrifice were performing a public service. But when they began charging exorbitant prices because they held a monopoly, they had moved from serving to exploiting the people, particularly the poor, who could ill afford their charges. Jesus' action was a form of social protest.

The most prominent recent example of the church's involvement in that kind of action was the civil rights movement of the 1960s, when church leaders across the country and across the theological spectrum said "enough." There has been discrimination, segregation, and second-class citizenship for persons of color long enough. Courageous pastors and lay people worked to register African-Americans to vote, worked to desegregate drinking fountains, public events, restaurants, movie houses, and a host of other previously segregated institutions. This, even in light of the fact that many churches remained, and still remain, segregated *de facto*. The church was right to be involved in that kind of political, social, and economic protest. There is almost universal agreement about that today. There is less agreement about more recent actions, such as the peace movement or the movement for equality of gays and lesbians.

Because there is not total agreement on an issue, however, does not mean the church should not take a stand. Morality, including social holiness, is the church's business. When we as the church take a stand, there are some guiding principles to which we need to pay attention. First and foremost, we need to know what we're talking about. It isn't enough to feel strongly about an issue. What are the facts? What is involved in an issue, and what do we need to know in order to take a stand? For example, the question about health insurance for poor children raised a great deal of heat on both sides of the argument in the Congress, the White House, and across the country. But what were the facts? Each side accused the other of distorting the truth. Each side accused the other of pushing political or personal agendas that had nothing to do with children's health insurance. For the church (us, since we are the church) to take a stand on an issue like that means that the church has to know what is really involved. In this example, who is uninsured? What are the specific needs of the uninsured population? What are the consequences of providing insurance for these children? What are the consequences if we don't? The list of questions could go on and on. Second, we need to speak clearly and calmly to make our views known. Third, it is important not to demonize those who disagree with us. Fourth, it is important to expect accountability from those we elect to represent us.

19

The Social Principles

● ●

From the days of John Wesley, United Methodists (and their predecessors) have had a deep concern for acts of justice. Noting that there were problems in social and economic systems, the church has worked to bring about changes in those systems. The emphasis has always been on ministry to and justice for the marginalized and the oppressed—those who did not have the power to bring about change for themselves. Wesley himself worked for prison reform, education reform, health care, the end of the slave trade, and many other issues, in addition to preaching and directing the work of the Revival in England. The American church, in its first Discipline, opposed slavery, though this was always a contentious issue.

In 1908 the Methodist Episcopal Church (North) adopted a social creed. That statement was basically supportive of the right of labor to organize to bargain collectively, a fairly radical position in 1908. The other bodies that now make up The

United Methodist Church followed suit, though not always on the same issue. In 1972, following the merger of The Methodist Church and The Evangelical United Brethren, the new church adopted a statement of Social Principles, a summary of the church's collective thought on the social, economic, and world conditions of the day. The Social Principles are compiled by the General Conference and they are the only official statement of The United Methodist Church on social issues. Any member of the church, or any agency, is free to disagree with the official position, and to speak to that disagreement, but what they say is not an official position of the church. Not even the Council of Bishops can speak for the church—only the General Conference can do that. The Social Principles are reviewed every four years by the General Conference and revised in the light of changing conditions in the world—and clearer understanding of moral and theological issues involved in speaking to the world.

In the Social Principles, the General Conference tries to speak to the church on contemporary issues based on their best understanding of Scripture and theology. The Social Principles are not church law, but an invitation to soul searching, careful study and action. No United Methodist has to agree with everything in The Social Principles—but it is expected that all United Methodists will take them seriously, even when they disagree.

There are broad categories of topics in the Social Principles. We will list those here and then take a deeper look at some positions on contemporary issues. Note that the Social Principles are open to revision in the light of new understandings, and some of the information here may be changed at a General Conference in 2008, 2012, or beyond.

1. The Natural World

This section deals with the environment, energy resources, animal life, space, science and technology, and food safety.

2. The Nurturing Community

Topics here include the family, other Christian communities, marriage, divorce, single persons, women and men, human sexuality, family violence and abuse, sexual harassment, abortion, adoption, faithful care of the dying, and suicide.

3. The Social Community

The rights of racial and ethnic persons, the rights of religious minorities, rights of children, rights of young people, the aging, women, persons with disabilities, equal rights regardless of sexual orientation, population, alcohol and other drugs, tobacco, medical experimentation, genetic technology, rural life, sustainable agriculture, urban-suburban life, media violence and Christian values, the internet, persons living with HIV and AIDS, the right to health care, and organ transplantation and donation.

4. The Economic Community

Topics here include property, collective bargaining, work and leisure, consumption, poverty, migrant workers, gambling, family farms, and corporate responsibility.

5. The Political Community.

Basic freedoms and human rights, political responsibility, freedom of information, education, civil obedience and civil disobedience, criminal and restorative justice, military service, are all topics covered here.

6. The World Community

Nations and cultures, war and peace, justice and law are topics touched on in this category.

With so many topics covered by the Social Principles, two points come immediately to mind. First, United Methodists obviously believe that the church belongs in a lot of places some of us would just as soon ignore. Second, it is almost guaranteed that we'll disagree with some of the positions the church takes on some topics somewhere in the Social Principles. That's OK, so long as we continue to think about them and dialogue with them.

It is also true that some of these positions will change in the future, as we get more and more information on a topic, or as new topics arise. For example, there is nothing in the Social Principles (as of this writing) about illegal immigration and very little about stem cell research, two hot topics in today's world. Nanotechnology is not even mentioned, though it will be a major scientific question in the near future. The statement on space is too vague, given the proliferation of human ventures into outer space. United Methodists—and the church—will continue to grow and develop understanding current issues in the light of the Scriptures and our own theological tradition. And, always, we will try to bring the best science (whether biology, economics, or sociology) to bear, along with the best knowledge of Scripture and theology.

Let's take some examples of the Social Principles as defined by the 2004 General Conference. We began this section by talking about recycling. The Social Principles has a brief reference to the reduction of municipal waste and the provision for "appropriate" recycling. One has to wonder what the General Conference meant by "appropriate." Drive down any major highway and you will see acres of abandoned motor vehicles, rusting in the weather. Some of them are being stripped for parts to be used in other vehicles, which would seem appropriate recycling. But what about the tons of metal and plastic sitting in these fields? Would it not be "appropriate" to encourage the development of technology for recycling those materials rather than let them simply fall into decay? Could that become a major new industry that would create jobs and save scarce resources? You see, raising those questions is an important discipline mentioned earlier in this book. The questions are "playing within the boundaries" laid down by the Social Principles, trying to define appropriate and search for new ways to apply the general principle to specific situations.

Did you know that the Social Principles have a stand on buying materials made in "conditions where workers are being exploited because of their age, gender, or economic status"? (The Social Principles, "Consumption" p. 116, 2004 *Book of Discipline*.) What if all United Methodists took that seriously and researched how the goods we buy are being made? Would we be willing to pay more for goods that are made within the guidelines suggested by the Social Principles? How might that make a difference in the world? What would be the "unintended consequences" of that action?

Those are only two areas where the Social Principles could call us, as a church and a nation, to new action. As in all ethical decisions, change in those areas would not come easily. We would have to study the situation carefully, consider the consequences (both intended and unintended) and then work constantly for change and accountability in the social and economic realms.

Calls for social holiness always raise the question, "What can we do? Nobody pays attention to little people like us." Jesus told a story about a judge who didn't care anything about God or the good opinion of his neighbors, and a poor widow who kept coming to him for justice in some small matter. He kept refusing her. She kept coming back. Finally, the judge gave her the justice she wanted, not because it was right, or because he had a change of heart and wanted to live out the commandments of the love of God and the love of neighbor. Nor did he do it because she had suddenly gained some power. No, he did it because she wouldn't let him alone. She was always "in his face" asking for the justice she deserved. That's the way we get things done. We stay on them. We keep getting "in the face" of elected officials, or company executives, until they finally do the right thing just to shut us up.

It's never easy being a Christian. In fact, it's hard work. But it is the task to which God calls us in the world.

Section IV Questions for Reflection

· ·

1. This section begins and ends with the statement, "It's not easy being a Christian." Is that statement true for you? What specific examples can you think of where being a Christian in the little details of daily life is hard? Why is it hard? What about your faith leads you to do it anyway?

2. Had you heard of The General Rules before? Have you ever read them? Your pastor or the church library has a copy in *The Book of Discipline*. Borrow a copy and read the General Rules for yourself. Then ask: what are some modern examples of the things Wesley was talking about? How could I add or change the examples here to make the General Rules fit my life?

3. Are the General Rules a guide for making decisions about personal and social morality? Why or why not?

4. What guidelines do you use when you make decisions on moral issues? How does the suggested list of guidelines in this section help you think of ways you could

deal with some ethical questions that have you puzzled?
5. When you talk about "big issues" in groups, how can your conversation be guided by Scripture, tradition, reason, experience?
6. How do you feel about the concept of "social holiness"? Does it resonate with anything you are struggling with in your life? How does the concept help you think about and deal with social issues?
7. Do the Social Principles, as they are described here, give you some guidelines for social holiness? Do they raise more questions for you? Is that a good thing?
8. Does "staying in their face" sound like a strategy for change? Why or why not?

FOR FURTHER READING

The Book of Discipline, published every four years by The United Methodist Publishing House. Read especially the sections, "The General Rules" and "The Social Principles."

Gooch, John O. *John Wesley for the 21st Century*. Nashville: Discipleship Resources, 2006. A look at Wesley's thought on a variety of social, economic, and political topics, with suggestions for how Wesley's thought can be a model for Christian life and action in today's world.

Yrigoyen, Jr., Charles. *John Wesley: Holiness of Heart and Life*. Nashville: Abingdon Press, 1996 A refreshing look at the concept of holiness as taught by John Wesley, and its relevance for today. A key chapter is on the topic of the holy life and the transformation of society.

Concluding Unscientific
Postscript

● ●

We began by saying that United Methodists were different from other denominations. As we've gone through the book, we've seen what some of the more important differences are. Contrary to the popular opinion that "you can believe anything and still be a Methodist," we've seen that there are some key doctrines that United Methodists historically (and still today) have held to. We've seen that United Methodists hold each other to account for our faith walk, our practices, even our beliefs. So, now that we've come this far, what do you think about your church?

Or, maybe, it's not your church. Maybe you picked up the book hoping to learn what United Methodism is all about. What have you read that intrigues you? What specific points would you like to know more about?

We began by talking about belonging, because most folks belong before they believe. Being a United Methodist means we belong to a particular institution, a part of the body of Christ. There are "secret handshakes," special vocabulary, and a unique history that make United Methodists who we are. How do you feel about the uniqueness of belonging?

Believing follows on the heels of belonging, so we explored doctrines that are emphasized by United Methodism. Those doctrines don't belong to us exclusively, but they are, as Wesley said, those with which God has particularly entrusted us. For the most part, United Methodist doctrines are a "middle way," providing a balance between the theological extremes growing out of late-medieval Roman Catholicism and the Reformation. The key doctrine for United Methodists is sanctification, also often called holiness or Christian perfection. It is the great Wesleyan contribution to Christian thought, and the challenge to all United Methodists to grow into perfection.

And that statement is a great segue into Growing. United Methodists believe that we are called to grow in both faith and action. We believe that God accepts us just as we are, but doesn't leave us to become comfortable where we are. So, we explored the doctrine of sanctification in some depth. To be honest, that is a doctrine with which many are uncomfortable. How can we expect to be perfect? But Christian perfection is a goal toward which we need to be striving. It is a doctrine that moves us beyond the comfort of much popular religion and makes us uneasy with less than the very best we can become, with the help of God. As tools for growing in faith, we looked at several kinds of spiritual disciplines—works of piety, works of mercy, and works of justice. So now the whole enterprise of growth comes down to you. How do you feel about God calling you to grow? To grow toward perfection? To commit yourself to spiritual disciplines that demand time and energy from you?

Finally, we talked about Living. What does it mean to be a Christian in practice? We looked at some templates for ethical decision-making, for dealing with the whole confused constellation of how one deals with right and wrong in the world. We talked about social ethics and social holiness, as well as personal ethics. The Social Principles of The United Methodist Church were lifted up as one way to look at secular issues from a sacred perspective. And, finally, we talked about where the church belongs, that is, what should the church, as an institution, be doing in the world? What do you believe about all that? To what would you be willing to commit yourself?

You see, being a Christian in the United Methodist tradition demands something from us. Belonging, believing, growing, and living are ways that often move us out of our comfort zones and call us to make a difference in the world. And we do that because we are disciples of Jesus Christ.